世界名著 英汉双语

常 识
Common Sense
译 注

[英] 托马斯·潘恩 著

杨宇冠 李 立 译

中国政法大学出版社

2016·北京

图书在版编目（ＣＩＰ）数据

常识译注/(英) 托马斯·潘恩 (Thomas Paine) 著；杨宇冠，李立译
北京：中国政法大学出版社，2016.9
　ISBN 978-7-5620-6918-8

　Ⅰ.①常…　Ⅱ.①托…　②杨…　③李…　Ⅲ.①政治思想史－美国－近代
Ⅳ.①D097.124

中国版本图书馆 CIP 数据核字 (2016) 第 220331 号

出 版 者	中国政法大学出版社
地　　址	北京市海淀区西土城路 25 号
邮寄地址	北京 100088 信箱 8034 分箱　邮编 100088
网　　址	http://www.cuplpress.com（网络实名：中国政法大学出版社)
电　　话	010-58908285（总编室）58908433（编辑部）58908334(邮购部)
承　　印	固安华明印业有限公司
开　　本	880mm×1230mm　1/32
印　　张	7.25
字　　数	130 千字
版　　次	2016 年 9 月第 1 版
印　　次	2016 年 9 月第 1 次印刷
定　　价	28.00 元

目录
CONTENTS

1776 年 1 月 9 日，托马斯·潘恩（Thomas Paine）出版了他的书《常识》[1]。作为一个从英国刚到北美洲不久的新移民，潘恩强烈宣传美国独立的主张，猛烈抨击英国的君主制，在当时引起轰动，起到推动美国独立的作用。《常识》原文只有 4 万多字，售价仅 18 便士，刚一上市就被抢购，卖出 15 万多册，各阶层的人争相阅读。[2]

托马斯·潘恩的《常识》，有若干不同的中文译本。笔者发现近几年就有十几个不同的译者的翻译本并由不同的出版社出版。一本小书，200 年后还能被人记得和提起，

---

[1] 在 1776 年 1 月出版的《常识》第一版中潘恩并未署自己的名字，而是以"一个英国人"的名义发行。《常识》出版后引起轰动，1776 年月 2 月，《常识》出版了第二版，仍然未署作者真名。潘恩在第二版的序言中表示，此书作者为谁并不重要，重要的是书中的思想内容。由于该书销量极好，同年又出版了第三版，潘恩在第三版中加写了后记，并署名托马斯·潘恩（Thomas Paine）。

[2] 参见［美］威廉·J. 本内特著，刘军等译：《美国通史》，江西人民出版社 2009 年版，第 68 页。

被不同的人翻译和出版，足见其是一本不同寻常的作品。

在阅读《常识》的中文本过程中，笔者还发现不同的中文本存在诸多差异〔3〕，与英文原文本也存在一定差异。为了读懂《常识》这本书，笔者对照阅读了《常识》的原文和部分中文本，并将笔者自己对英文原文的理解记录下来，从而形成了自己的"译本"。为加深对这本书的理解，笔者在阅读过程中还把书中涉及的各个人物、事件等背景知识以译者注的形式加在每页的脚注之中，并把与这本书相关的一些历史文件附录在本书之后，从而形成了这本《常识译注》。

原以为阅读和翻译这本小书会很快完成，可是动手之后，才意识到不太容易，不仅有许多背景知识需要了解，而且有些英文表述需要经过反复琢磨才能理解。从 2015 年 10 月至 2016 年 1 月 9 日，经过两个多月时间，才完成了翻译这本小书的译注初稿，后来又修改了很多次。在《常识》的后记部分译完之后，我发现历史上的今天，1776 年 1 月 9 日是《常识》第一版问世的时候，至今正是 240 周年。这当然只是巧合。

---

〔3〕 例如在关于潘恩国籍问题上，就有不同说法，曾尔恕等人翻译的《常识》封面上注明潘恩为英国籍；李芳华翻译的《常识》封面注明潘恩为美国籍。实际上，在 1776 年《常识》刚出版时，美国还没有成立，潘恩也自称"一个英国人"，所以作者应当是英国籍。但是，由于潘恩在《常识》中强烈呼吁美国独立，猛烈抨击英国的政治制度和英国国王，完全站在美国的立场，似乎他已经不是英国人。后来他在法国被监禁时，英国和美国都没有对他提供领事保护。本书根据潘恩写作和诸次发表《常识》时自称的国籍，将其作为英国人。

一、潘恩生平

托马斯·潘恩于 1737 年 1 月 29 日出生在英国诺福克郡（Norfolk）一个贫苦人家。父亲是英格兰诺福克郡一名穷苦的制衣匠人。幼年时，潘恩就失学了，因为生活困难，他很早就参加工作，先后做过店员、裁缝（据说专做胸衣）、教员、税吏、海员等职业，但都做得不如意。他曾经两次结婚，但是婚姻也不成功，均以离异告终，似乎也没有留下子女。在《常识》发表之前，他一直把自己的姓写成"Pain"（痛苦），以示对英国社会的抗议。潘恩的事业和家庭受到诸多挫折，可能与其性格倔强、直率和激进有关。他是个"善善恶恶"的人，但是 18 世纪的英国社会，他"善善不能举，恶恶不能去"，从而四面树敌，度日艰难。然而他并不因此而屈服，而是把个人的痛苦和社会的不平等诉诸笔端，他当税吏时写了小册子《税吏事件》，描写英国税吏的苦恼。1774 年 4 月，他因有"反政府"思想被免职。

潘恩虽然学历不高，但言辞犀利，对当时英国社会抨击激烈，逐渐小有名气。1774 年潘恩经本杰明·富兰克林[4]

---

〔4〕　本杰明·富兰克林（Benjamin Franklin，1706～1790）出生于美国马萨诸塞州波士顿，美国著名政治家、物理学家，同时亦是出版商、印刷商、记者、作家、慈善家、外交家及发明家。他是美国独立战争时重要的领导人之一，参与了多项重要文件的草拟，并曾出任美国驻法国大使，成功取得法国对美国

介绍到北美洲，[5] 在费城担任《宾夕法尼亚》杂志的编辑。当时，正值北美人民反英斗争风起云涌，但是，人们还没有公开提出反对英国国王和美国独立，当时许多人的君主制观念还根深蒂固，连华盛顿、富兰克林、亚当斯这些独立战争时期著名的政治家，都没有明确提出美国独立。就在这样的形势下，1776 年初潘恩发表了影响深远的激进小册子《常识》，公开提出美国独立革命的问题，并竭力强调革命之后建立共和政体才是该书的宗旨所在。《常识》一出，立刻席卷北美大陆，引起巨大反响，成了美国独立革命的教科书。

潘恩也身体力行参与了美国独立和建国的工作，他曾经参加过美国军队，在前线作战的潘恩写下数篇战斗檄文，鼓舞士气。潘恩也曾在大陆会议外交委员会（the Committee of Foreign Affairs）工作，但他最主要的贡献在于写作政论文章。

潘恩的主要著作有：《常识》《美国危机》《理性时代》《人权论》《土地正义论》，其中以《常识》和《人权论》最为著名。潘恩《常识》中痛斥英国世袭君主的罪恶

（接上页）独立的支持。1757 年，富兰克林代表宾夕法尼亚州到英国向英王陈述，在英国居住了五年，这期间向英国人民及政府官员阐述了殖民地的状况和意见。他也曾负责殖民地外事事务，常常到英国和欧洲大陆各国，在英国期间与潘恩结识。

〔5〕［美］艾伦·布林克利著，邵旭东译：《美国史》，海南出版社 2009 年版，第 126 页。

和对北美洲殖民地的种种压迫和掠夺，大声疾呼号召美国独立。他论证了美利坚独立的必要性和可行性，设想了独立后的美国国体、政体等相关问题。潘恩这本书，成了独立战争时期人民大众的教科书，出版不久销量即达到 10 余万册〔6〕，这在当时是一个巨大的数字，在出版界的历史上也算是数量很多的了。潘恩的这本《常识》强有力地影响了美利坚的舆论，为美国独立起到了难以估量的推动作用。

在美国独立战争〔7〕过程中，潘恩继续发挥他写作的特长，写下一系列论美国危机的文章。但是，在美国已经独立之后，潘恩为美国独立大声疾呼的作用已经完成，他在新政府中却没有得到重要的职位，在经济上似乎也没有得到优厚的待遇。1783 年在英国承认美国独立之后，美国独立战争结束，美国与原来的宗主国英国之间因为独立而

---

〔6〕 潘恩的《常识》在当时的销量有不同说法。据《美国史》记载，"《常识》出版的前几个月就售出 10 余万册（考虑到当时的美国人口，这个数字相当于今天在美国 800 万册的发行量。"参见 ［美］艾伦·布林克利著，邵旭东译：《美国史》，海南出版社 2009 年版，第 126 页。

〔7〕 美国独立战争，（American Revolutionary War，1775～1783），或称美国革命战争。始于 1775 年 4 月的莱克星顿枪战案，1776 年 7 月 4 日大陆会议通过了由托马斯·杰斐逊执笔起草的《独立宣言》，宣告了美国的诞生。在战争中，英国能够利用他们在海军上的优势以占领殖民地的临海城市，但如何控制乡村地区却使他们困惑。经过北美人民的艰苦抗争，英美终于在 1783 年 9 月 3 日签订《巴黎和约》，英国承认美国独立。美国独立战争结束了英国的殖民统治，实现了国家的独立，确立了比较民主的资产阶级政治体制，有利于美国资本主义的发展，对以后欧洲和拉丁美洲的革命起到了推动作用。

产生的冲突已经告一段落，在建设美国的过程中，华盛顿等领导者着手与英国发展友好关系，再鼓动与英国斗争已经不合时宜。作为职业革命家，本来并不因为个人利益而革命，然而对一般人而言，革命成功之后，未能享受高官厚禄，失落也许是难免的。潘恩失去了攻击的靶子，他曾经致力于工程发明。然而当时的美国人才济济，富兰克林就是大发明家。潘恩的发明在美国也似乎未能得到重视。

美国独立之后，欧洲的革命正方兴未艾。1787 年，潘恩返回欧洲。潘恩回到英国之后，他并未因撰写《常识》，鼓吹美国独立，攻击英国政府和国王而受到追究和迫害。作为革命家，他继续抨击英国君主立宪政体，撰写文章支持革命。1791 年 3 月，他在伦敦出版《人权论》，激烈抨击柏克的《法国革命论》〔8〕，引起英吉利海峡两岸舆论界的轰动，并给当时还处于摸索状态的法国大革命〔9〕指明

〔8〕 柏克（Edmund Burke，1729～1797）是 18 世纪下半叶英国的政治理论家，《法国革命论》是他最享负盛名的一部作品，书中对法国大革命持反对观点。

〔9〕 法国大革命（1789～1799）是发生在法国推翻旧制度的一场革命，也是人类历史上一场激烈的政治及社会变革，在受到赞扬的同时，也因革命期间出现的一些暴力行为而为人诟病。在这一场革命中，许多人失去了生命，包括法兰西国王路易十六和王后，以及杰出科学家和许多普通的百姓。法国大革命的旗号是反专制独裁，争取民主、自由、人权，但在革命中一些领导人自己走向了专制，许多曾经高喊保障自由、博爱、人权而奋斗的人在革命中使用暴力残害别人或受到别人迫害。法国大革命的一些知名的领导人，还有很多不知名的人，他们曾经积极投身革命之中，没有死于和敌人的斗争之中，最终却被"自己人"在这场革命中杀害。这种现象称为："革命吞噬了自己的孩子。"（La révolution dévore ses enfants）

了共和主义的方向。潘恩的这些学说在当时君主制统治下的英国还不流行，甚至引起一些人的反感和指责。1792年6月，英国政府煽动一些人反对潘恩，并意图指控他犯有煽动叛乱罪。潘恩临危不惧，仍然宣传他的革命思想和主张。

1792年9月13日，潘恩的友人获悉警方在密谋逮捕潘恩，于是极力劝说潘恩立即逃亡，否则便有杀身之祸。潘恩初意不走，后经英国和法国朋友们的恳切劝说，终于同意连夜流亡法国。9月13日，当潘恩踏上法国土地时，受到人们热烈欢迎。9月19日，潘恩抵达巴黎。20日晚，进入法国议会。1792年10月11日，法国国民公会选举组成起草新宪法的九人小组，潘恩光荣入选。从此，他又投身法国大革命中。

他参与《法国1793宪法中的人权宣言》〔10〕的制定。该《宣言》再次确认和完善了《1789年法国人权和公民权宣言》〔11〕的内容，成为新的具有宪法意义的《法国人权宣言》，其内容反映了潘恩的人权思想并与《美国独立宣言》和美国《权利法案》〔12〕交相辉映，对后世人权保障国际文

---

〔10〕《法国1793宪法中的人权宣言》是法国大革命期间通过的人权宣言，全文共35条，中文译本参见董云虎编著：《人权基本文献要览》，辽宁人民出版社1994年版。

〔11〕 通常称《法国人权和公民权宣言》，它是法国大革命爆发后由国民议会宣布法国大革命原则的著名文件。中文译本参见董云虎编著：《人权基本文献要览》，辽宁人民出版社1994年版。

〔12〕《美国独立宣言》见本书附录。

件产生了长期和深远的影响〔13〕。

随着法国大革命愈演愈烈，潘恩与雅各宾派之间出现了隔阂。潘恩不懂法语，与他交往的人大多数是能说英语的吉伦特派〔14〕人士，这些人中有一些人早年参加过北美独立战争，与潘恩意气相投。而法国大革命中的雅各宾派〔15〕多是一些法国外省人，很少有人说英语。潘恩在法国的朋友布里索〔16〕、罗兰夫妇〔17〕等吉伦特派领袖与大革命中的

〔13〕 1948 年联合国制定的《世界人权宣言》，1950 年欧洲理事会制定的《欧洲人权公约》和 1966 年联合国制定的《公民及政治权利国际盟约》等国际人权文件中都采纳了《美国独立宣言》和《法国人权宣言》中的一些内容。

〔14〕 吉伦特派（Girondin），因是布里索（Jacques - Pierre Brissot）的追随者，原称布里索派（Brissotin），后因其中很多人原是吉伦特省人，因此又被称为吉伦特派。

〔15〕 雅各宾派是法国大革命时期参加雅各宾俱乐部的资产阶级激进派政治团体，成员大多数是小业主。主要领导人有罗伯斯庇尔、丹东、马拉、圣茹斯特等。

〔16〕 雅克 - 皮埃尔·布里索（Jacques - Pierre Brissot，1754 ~ 1793）法国政治家、记者。法国大革命期间吉伦特派领袖。早年当过律师事务所职员。曾因出版反对专制政体的小册子而被囚禁。后去英国旅行。在英国曾为《欧洲通讯》编辑部撰稿。1788 年 2 月创立黑人之友社，主张有色人种权利平等。同年 5 月赴美，1789 年回国后创办《法兰西爱国者》报。后参加雅各宾俱乐部，被选入立法议会和国民公会。主张废除君主制，建立共和国。他是立法议会中吉伦特派的领导人，促使法国于 1792 年 4 月对奥地利宣战。在吉伦特派掌权期间，他主张对内实行联邦制，对外进行扩张。在他主持外交委员会时，法国于 1793 年 2 月 ~ 3 月对英国、荷兰宣战。他的政治主张遭到罗伯斯庇尔和山岳派的反对。1792 年 10 月 10 日被逐出雅各宾俱乐部。1793 年吉伦特派政权被推翻后，布里索在逃亡中被捕，经革命法庭判处死刑。

〔17〕 罗兰夫人（Manon Jeanne Phlipon，1754 年 3 月 17 日 ~ 1793 年 11 月 8 日），法国大革命时期著名的政治家。吉伦特党领导人之一。她的丈夫罗兰（Jean Marie Roland de la Platiere）也是吉伦特党的领导人之一。罗兰夫人于 1793 年 11 月 8 日被雅各宾派送上断头台。临刑前在她留下了一句为后人所熟知的

雅各宾派意见不同，受到残酷镇压，潘恩与他们交好，也受到了牵连。

在对法国国王路易十六[18]审判案的态度方面，潘恩与雅各宾派发生冲突。潘恩不忘路易十六在北美战争中对美国的援助。他认为法国革命不在于与一个国王作对，而是与产生国王的那种制度作战。潘恩虽然认为国王应该废黜，昏君通敌亦必须惩办，但只宜流放，不宜处死，他担心处死国王可能伤害美国盟友的感情[19]和激起欧洲王室的联合干涉。1793年1月15日，在国民公会中对法国国王路易十六审判的公开投票中[20]，潘恩投票反对处死国王。

继法国国王案件问题之后，他又在法制溃坏、限价风潮

（接上页）名言："O Liberté, que de crimes on commet en ton nom!"（自由，多少罪恶假汝之名以行！）

　　[18]　路易十六（Louis XVI，1754年8月23日～1793年1月21日，享年38岁），是波旁王朝国王（1774年～1792年在位），路易十五之孙，法兰西波旁王朝复辟前最后一任国王，也是欧洲历史中第二个被处死的国王。

　　[19]　法国由于历史上与英国的矛盾，特别是在争夺北美殖民地问题上与英国有利害冲突，法国国王路易十六国王对美国独立很支持，所以美国人对路易十六国王颇有好感。1790年，莫里斯在致华盛顿的信中还提到："路易十六是一位慈祥厚道的人，是一个绝好的太平宰相。"参见［法］马德楞著，伍光建译：《法国大革命史》，人民日报出版社2014年版，第24页。

　　[20]　如何处理国王，国民公会代表存在激烈争论，集中在下列问题：路易十六是否拥有不可侵犯权、国民公会是否有权变为法庭、审判路易十六对共和国有没有好处。在封建时代，国王地位至高无上，神圣不可侵犯，绝对不受司法审判。审判国王，于法不合。吉伦特派希望拖延审判，雅各宾派主张处死国王。有人主张由法院裁决，其他代表则强调，国民公会足以代表法国民意，由全体代表审判国王。12月3日法国国民公会通过决议，宣布由国民公会对路易十六进行公审，由议员当场唱名表决。

等问题上与雅各宾派发生矛盾。罗伯斯庇尔 [21] 最初对潘恩很有好感，读过他的《常识》《人权论》等著作后，以他为知己同道。可是当与潘恩共事后不久，他就发现潘恩并不是一个无套裤汉 [22] ，结果大失所望，反目成仇。雅各宾派在法国大革命中非常激进，对持不同意见者残酷镇压。潘恩作为理想主义者，也不愿放弃自己的见解。

1793 年春发生马拉被刺杀的案件 [23] ，潘恩出庭作

---

〔21〕 马克西米连·佛朗索瓦·马里·伊西多·德·罗伯斯庇尔，（又译为罗伯斯比尔，罗伯斯比，Maximilien François Marie Isidore de Robespierre，1758 年 5 月 6 日 ~1794 年 7 月 28 日），法国革命家，法国大革命时期重要的领袖人物，是雅各宾派政府的实际首脑之一。在他执政后期，改组革命法庭，简化审判程序，实行雅各宾专政，以革命的恐怖政策惩罚罪犯和革命的叛徒，许多无辜的人都被诬告并被杀害，成千上万的人被送上断头台，最后罗伯斯庇尔自己也在法国大革命中被判处死刑。

〔22〕 无套裤汉（法语：sans – culotte）。无套裤汉的主要成分是小手工业者、小商贩、小店主和其他劳动群众，也包括一些富人。当时法国贵族男子盛行穿紧身短套裤，膝盖以下穿长筒袜；平民则穿长裤，无套裤，故有无套裤汉之称。无套裤汉原是贵族对平民的讥称，但不久成为革命者的同义语。他们是城市革命的主力军，是大革命中几次武装起义的参加者。在推翻王政、建立共和国以及推动雅各宾派实行恐怖统治，抗击外国武装干涉等方面发挥了极大作用。

〔23〕 马拉全名让·保尔·马拉（Jean Paul Marat，1743 ~1793 年），法国政治家、医生，法国大革命时期民主派革命家。1789 年大革命爆发后，马拉即投入战斗，是雅各宾派的重要成员。他创办的《人民之友报》，成为支持激进民主措施的喉舌。他猛烈抨击当权的君主立宪派的温和政策，要求建立民主制度，消灭贫富悬殊的社会状况，反对富有者的统治，尊重穷苦人的地位。1793 年 7 月 13 日马拉在巴黎寓所中被夏洛蒂·科黛刺杀。马拉之死震动了整个法国。科黛出身于没落贵族家庭，在修道院里长大并接受教育，性格有些孤寂离群。从法国大革命开始，科黛就成为彻底的共和主义者，但随着革命一步步走向毫无节制的恐怖和杀戮，科黛开始失望和怀疑，最终导致她刺杀了法国大革命中著名领导人马拉。科黛旋即被捕并交付审判，当天就被判处死刑。

证。在该案审理中揭发了马拉的隐私，激恼雅各宾派。6月，雅各宾派正式执政。潘恩当年的朋友或被处死或逃亡。同年10月，潘恩的名字也上了镇压的名单。11月25日，罗伯斯庇尔公布取缔外籍议员的法令，潘恩被逐出国民公会。紧接着，罗伯斯庇尔又亲自批准逮捕和起诉潘恩。12月28日深夜，潘恩被捕入狱。在当时的政治环境下，被捕之后很可能被判死刑而被处决。但是，罗伯斯庇尔还未来得及处决潘恩，自己就被推翻并被判处死刑立即执行，潘恩侥幸逃得一命。

潘恩在法国被关押在狱达10个月之久。这期间英国政府由于对他的仇视而对其进行了缺席审判，判决潘恩为非法之人。英国政府对于潘恩在法国被关押之事不提出交涉，故意造成潘恩已经不是英国的国民，不享受英国领事保护的印象。当时潘恩曾向美国求援，要求证实他有美国国籍。但是，据说美国驻法国大使莫里斯因为与潘恩有私怨〔24〕，不肯证明他具有美国国籍，华盛顿也对他不提供

---

〔24〕 莫里斯（Gouverneur Morris，1752年1月31日~1816年11月6日）美国政治家，美国建国元勋之一，美国宪法的主要起草人和签字人。1781年至1785年在费城任财产主管。1789年到法国办理业务，1792年至1794年出任美国驻法国大使。潘恩在美国任大陆会议外交事务委员会秘书期间曾公开揭露美利坚与法国交往中一些人谋取私利的丑闻，引起莫里斯不满。法国驻北美使节向大陆会议抗议潘恩暴露了法国军援的秘密，要求大陆会议"对目前的状况采取合适的措施"。1779年2月9日，潘恩被迫提出辞呈。因此，莫里斯与潘恩两人产生矛盾。

任何帮助和保护，听任他在法国被关押，差一点被杀死。[25]

1794年8月，门罗[26]代替莫里斯，出使法国。他惊讶地获悉潘恩还在法国监狱中，遂四处奔走，火速营救，1794年11月7日，在门罗多方斡旋之后，潘恩终于获释出狱。潘恩出狱后，拿破仑[27]曾访问过他，但拿破仑在执政后，与潘恩的关系迅速冷却下来，因为潘恩厌弃君主制和个人独裁，拒绝与拿破仑合作。同年，他在美国发表了著作《理性时代》（*The Age of Reason*），文章中对基督教展开强烈质疑。

1801年，杰弗逊就任美国总统。1802年9月，杰弗逊邀请潘恩回到美国。其时美国已经立国，潘恩关于美国独

---

〔25〕 参见［法］马德楞著，伍光建译：《法国大革命史》，人民日报出版社2014年版，其中记载："英人佩因（Paine）倡自由民权之说，避祸至北美时，英、美不相能，佩因复至英，法国人慕其名，三省先后争举为议员。新议员卢未（Louvet）善著小说，以辞令闻，为书劝佩因行。佩因遂至巴黎。及处置路易问题发生时，佩因不主张判死罪，为罗伯斯庇尔所疑，因于刑部大监，狱卒见牢门无号数，未拽之赴法场，竟幸免于杀。"

〔26〕 詹姆斯·门罗（James Monroe，1758年4月28日~1831年7月4日），美国资产阶级民主派，美国第5任总统，美国对拉美政策的主要奠基人，即门罗主义的制订人。同时，詹姆斯·门罗也是一位卓越的外交家，对美利坚合众国的外交事业主要体现于他的《就职演说辞》和《门罗宣言》中。当政时的美国和平稳定、繁荣昌盛、版图扩大，因而赢得了"和谐时代"的美名。

〔27〕 拿破仑·波拿巴（法语：Napoléon Bonaparte，1769年8月15日~1821年5月5日），即拿破仑一世（Napoléon I），出生于科西嘉岛，19世纪著名军事家、政治家，法兰西第一帝国的缔造者。法兰西第一共和国第一执政（1799年~1804年），法兰西第一帝国皇帝（1804年~1815年）。

立的宣传和建国的设想已经实现而成为过去。当时正处于宗教复兴期间，潘恩的那本《理性时代》给他带来了很大麻烦，受到许多人的攻击。

1809 年 6 月 8 日，潘恩在孤苦无告中于美国纽约辞世，享年 72 岁。潘恩是美国独立战争时期的启蒙思想家、激进的革命者，为美国的独立革命做出了巨大的贡献，曾被视为美国开国元勋之一，为此得罪了英国政府；他参加法国大革命，因与雅各宾派不合，身陷牢狱，差点失去生命；回到美国之后，又因攻击宗教而受到迫害。一生遭际，令人不胜唏嘘。

二、《常识》的历史背景

《常识》发表于美国独立前夕。美国全称为美利坚合众国（The United States of America），现在是由华盛顿哥伦比亚特区、50 个州和关岛等众多海外领土组成的联邦共和立宪制国家。其主体部分位于北美洲中部。美国是移民国家，在哥伦布发现新大陆时，居住在美洲的印第安人，其中有大约 100 多万人居住在现在的加拿大和美国中北部，这片辽阔土地上只有如此少量的印第安人原住民，大部分是未开发的地方，称之为"新大陆"。

英国是最早向北美洲移民的国家之一。1607 年一批英国移民来到北美，建立了詹姆士镇（Jamestown），这是英国在北美所建立的第一个永久性殖民地。17 世纪初，英国开始向北美殖民。最初的北美移民主要是一些失去土地的农民、生活艰苦的工人以及受宗教迫害的清教徒。1620年，他们乘"五月花号"（May Flower）前往北美并在船上制定《五月花号公约》[28]。在 11 月 21 日于普利茅斯上岸，清教徒中的 41 名成年男人签署共同遵守《五月花号公约》（The May Flower Compacts）。内容为组织公民团体，拟订法规等。奠定了自治政府的基础。

1630 年大约 700 名清教徒搭乘 11 只船从英国前往马萨诸塞。1642 年有两万人前往新英格兰。这些人不畏艰难

---

〔28〕 五月花号（May Flower）是英国移民驶往北美的一艘最为著名的船只。船上的人是一些英国清教徒和他们的家属。这些英国清教徒来自英国东北部，由于在英国受到残酷迫害，于 1608 年逃往荷兰，但发现生活很困难，为找寻适合自己的土地和自由信仰自己的宗教，他们于 1620 年 9 月乘"五月花号"客船前往北美。同船的 102 名移民中有三分之一是清教徒，其余的人是伦敦商人托马斯·韦斯顿（Thomas Weston）的雇工。经过九个星期的海上航行，他们于当年 11 月到达科德角（今马萨诸塞州普罗文斯敦），于感恩节后的第一天在普利茅斯上岸。为了平息移民者在航行中积累的纠纷，也为了上岸建立新殖民地以及可能的自治政府作好准备。1620 年 11 月 11 日，五月花号船上 102 名新移民中的 41 名清教徒成年男子签署了《五月花号公约》。这份公约成为美国日后无数自治公约中的首例，它的签约方式及内容代表着"人民可以由自己的意思来决定自治管理的方式，不再由人民以上的强权来决定管理"。在此开创了一个自我管理的社会结构，这在王权与神权统治的时代，暗示了许多民主的信念。《五月花号公约》写道："为了上帝的荣耀，为了增加基督教的信仰，为了提高我们国王和国家的荣耀，我们漂洋过海，在弗吉尼亚北部开发第一个殖民地。我们这些签署人在上帝面前共同庄严立誓签约，自愿结为民众自治团体。为了使上述目地能得到更好的实施、维护和发展，将来不时依此而制定颁布，被认为是对这殖民地全体人民都最合适、最方便的法律、法规、条令、宪章和公职，我们都保证遵守和服从。"

险阻，离开英国前往新大陆，就是为了摆脱宗教压迫和查理一世〔29〕统治下英国的经济状况。从1607年到1733年，英国殖民者先后在北美洲东岸（大西洋沿岸）建立了十三个殖民地。在18世纪中期，殖民地的经济、文化、政治相对成熟，殖民地议会仍臣服英王乔治三世〔30〕，不过他们追求与英国议会同等的地位，并不想成为英国的次等公民。但是，此时英法之间的七年战争结束，英国急于巩固领土，便向北美殖民地人民征收重税，同时英王乔治三世主张高压手段。因此，引发殖民地人民的反抗。

---

〔29〕 查理一世（Charles I，又译查尔斯一世，1600年11月19日~1649年1月30日）自1625年3月27日起至1649年1月30日被处死（他是唯一的以国王身份被处死的英格兰国王），他担任英格兰、苏格兰及爱尔兰国王。查理一世在位期间英国信仰混乱，宗教冲突严重，臣民们普遍对他们国王的信仰持不信任态度。在查理一世最后的几年中，他与国会之间爆发了英国内战。同时他又制定了一系列的宗教政策，引起了以清教徒为代表的加尔文教派的不满。查理一世在第一次英国内战（1642~1645）中被击败后，议会希望他能够接受君主立宪制。然而查理一世执迷不悟，他与苏格兰结盟，并逃到了怀特岛郡，这种行为彻底激怒了国会，从而导致了第二次英国内战（1648~1649）。查理一世再一次被击败，随后他被捕，审判，定罪，并以叛国罪被处死。

〔30〕 乔治三世（George Ⅲ，1738年6月4日~1820年1月29日），全名乔治·威廉·弗雷德里克（George William Frederick），1760年10月25日登基为大不列颠国王及爱尔兰国王，至1801年1月1日后因大不列颠及爱尔兰组成联合王国而成为联合王国国王，直到1820年死亡为止。乔治三世漫长的统治，见证了其王国与大片欧洲大陆进行的一连串军事冲突。在他的统治初期，大不列颠在七年战争中击败法国，并使大不列颠压倒欧洲各国，成功支配着北美洲及印度地区。随着大不列颠在美国独立战争的战败，乔治三世在北美洲失去了大量殖民地，这些殖民地的独立最终促成美国立国。此后，乔治三世参与了一连串的反法战争，反抗拿破仑及革命后的法国，这些战争最后以拿破仑在1815年于滑铁卢被击败而结束。

自从英国在美洲建立殖民地，英国与殖民地之间的裂痕也就开始了。起初，英国政府建立了许多机构管理美洲殖民地事务，英国议会通过适用于殖民地的各种法律，英国的外交官决定殖民地与其他国家的关系。但是，由于地理分隔遥远和利益不同，殖民地的一些业主、公司及一些居民都发现在殖民地内部创建当地政府处理日常事务更为便利。1619 年 7 月 30 日，弗吉尼亚率先成立了市民议会（The Virginia General Assembly），这是新大陆最早的立法机构，由上下两院组成，共有 140 名由该地各区平均选举的代表。到 1700 年，北美各殖民地都建立了自己的立法机构。

18 世纪中叶，北美殖民地和宗主国英国之间的矛盾日益尖锐。为加强殖民统治，英国政府不但颁布了一系列税法，还颁布了《驻军法案》（Quartering Act，又称"驻营条例"）和《唐森德法案》（Townshend Acts）。《唐森德法案》是 1767 年英国国会通过的向北美殖民地征税的法案，由财政大臣唐森德[31]（又译名为"汤森"）提出，故名又《唐森德税法》。为了征收税款，当时英国关税税吏有权闯入殖民地民宅、货栈、店铺，搜查违禁物品和走私货物。唐森德认为，"只要英王和议会拥有至高无上的主权，美洲

---

　　〔31〕唐森德（Charles Townshend，1725 年 8 月 28 日～1767 年 9 月 4 日），又译为"汤森"，英国政治家，曾任英国财政大臣，主持制定了《1767 年唐森德税法》，引起殖民地人民愤怒，加剧了殖民地与英国的矛盾。

人就必须纳税。一旦殖民地人民习惯于支持这些商品的关税之后，征税货物名单就可能被拉长。"[32]英国对北美殖民地的经济压榨与政治统治，激起当地人民强烈反抗。

弗吉尼亚议会在杰斐逊的领导下呼吁各殖民地联合起来共同斗争，建议召开由各殖民地代表参加的会议，共同"商讨各殖民地的不幸的现状"。1774 年 9 月 5 日到 10 月 26 日，在费城召开了殖民地联合会议，史称"第一届大陆会议"（First Continental Congress）。除佐治亚缺席外，其他 12 个殖民地的 55 名代表都参加了会议。大陆会议的核心问题是如何与英国对抗。大会制定了"经济抵制计划"，后来形成了"美洲大陆联合会"（Continental Association），规定联合会成员不得进口和消费英国货，如果英国议会不退让的话，还禁止殖民地的产品出口到英国。联合会还号召每一个美洲人社区建立本地的监察和检查委员会，敦促所有居民都参与抵制英国的活动。大会要求英国没有得到殖民地人民的同意就不得向殖民地征税，要求殖民地实行自治，撤走英国驻军。如果英国不接受这些要求，北美殖民地将于 12 月 1 日起抵制英货，同时禁止将任何商品输往英国。这些活动逐渐演化为美国独立革命。

北美的独立运动还有两个原因：新英格兰商人要求对

---

〔32〕 ［美］詹姆斯·柯比等著，范道丰等译：《美国史》上册，商务印书馆 2012 年版，第 159 页。

外贸易的自由〔33〕，和以弗吉尼亚为首的南方种植园主对
西部的土地要求。最初的反抗源于新英格兰商人们反对英
国议会的无端加税，英国殖民当局对此处理不当，最后不
得不驻军波士顿。到了1774年，驻军达十一个团。这时
幕后指挥波士顿人民反抗英国殖民当局的塞缪尔·亚当
斯〔34〕，觉得单靠波士顿和马萨诸塞的力量已无法应付了，
有必要召开北美所有殖民地参加的会议来讨论当前的局
势。在亚当斯的倡议下，马萨诸塞议会通过决议，决定召
开北美各殖民地的代表大会，并由议会的通信委员会出面
通知各殖民地议会。决议在6月17日通过后，马萨诸塞的
英国总督盖奇解散了议会。稍早一些，弗吉尼亚的英国总
督反对民选议会，解散了弗吉尼亚议会。被解散的弗吉尼
亚议会在威廉斯堡开会，5月27日，通过了召开有13个
殖民地参加的会议的决议。在马萨诸塞和弗吉尼亚的号召
下，除乔治亚以外的12个北美殖民地的55位代表于1774
年9月5日，在费城召开了第一届大陆会议。第一届大陆
会议向英国递交了请愿书，要求取消对各殖民地的强硬措

---

〔33〕 早在美国《独立宣言》发表之前，大陆会议就曾派代表到欧洲各国
洽谈商业协定。这些协定自然要求美国成为一个独立主权的国家。

〔34〕 塞缪尔·亚当斯（Samuel Adams，1722年9月27日~1803年10月2
日），美国革命家、政治家，马萨诸塞州人。生于波士顿，毕业于哈佛大学。他
积极参加革命活动，是自由之子的创建者之一和领导人，他领导了反对《食糖
法》《印花税法》《唐森德税法》等英国针对美洲殖民地的法律的运动，策动波
士顿倾茶事件，是美国《独立宣言》的签署人之一。

施。会议还通过了与英国断绝贸易关系的决议。

第一届大陆会议之后，英王变本加厉地对殖民地采取镇压措施，引起了 1775 年 4 月 19 日列克星敦的武装冲突。在人民反英武装斗争和高涨的革命情绪推动下，1775 年 5 月 10 日，第二届大陆会议在费城召开。与会代表 66 人；新代表中有本杰明·富兰克林和托马斯·杰斐逊〔35〕。约翰·汉考克〔36〕被选为会议主席。在反英革命战争事业已开始的情况下，大陆会议在性质上来说，已发展为国家政权组织，开始起着常设中央政府的作用。大会开始时争论的焦点集中在组建大陆军队的问题上。会议于 1775 年 6 月 15 日通过组织大陆军和任命华盛顿为总司令的决议，代表们赞成利用波士顿周围的爱国力量组成大陆军队，并要求其他殖民地招募新兵。在代表们中的一些温和派〔37〕要求下，大陆会议通过《关于拿起武器的原因和必要性的公

〔35〕 托马斯·杰斐逊（Thomas Jefferson，1743 年 4 月 13 日～1826 年 7 月 4 日），美国第三任总统（1801～1809），《美国独立宣言》主要起草人，美国开国元勋中最具影响力者之一。除了政治事业外，杰斐逊同时也是农业学、园艺学、建筑学、词源学、考古学、数学、密码学、测量学与古生物学等学科的专家，又身兼作家、律师与小提琴手，也是弗吉尼亚大学的创办人。

〔36〕 约翰·汉考克（John Hancock，1737 年 1 月 12 日～1793 年 10 月 8 日），美国革命家、政治家，富商出身。是独立宣言的第一个签署人。由于他在宣言上高贵的亲笔签名，英文中"约翰·汉考克"成为亲笔签名的代名词。

〔37〕 温和派都是一些保守人士，尽管他们十分关心美洲人的权利，但却害怕独立。像许多其他富有的殖民地人士一样，他们担心没有英国稳定的统治，殖民地内部可能会混乱起来。他们还怀疑一个脆弱、独立的美洲国家，周围都是雄心勃勃的欧洲国家，是否能长期生存下来。参见：〔美〕詹姆斯·柯比等著，范道丰等译：《美国史》上册，商务印书馆 2012 年版，第 126 页。

告》，向英国政府说明殖民地组建军队的目的，并不是想要"解除在我们之间如此长久而幸福地存在着的那一联合"，而是确保美洲人的生命、自由和财产。

英国政府漠视美洲各殖民地的要求，拒绝殖民地的请愿，反对各殖民地独立。1775 年 10 月 27 日，英国国王乔治三世对英国议会发表演说，表明英国"不能放弃这些诸多殖民地，英国开拓了这些殖民地的工业，养育了这些殖民地，给予诸多商业优惠，并花费巨大生命和财产的牺牲保护它们的安全"。国王提出要"以决断的方法迅捷结束动乱。为此，增加了海军力量，扩大了我们地面军力"。在这种情况下，殖民地人民面临着多种选择，继续屈从英国的统治与英国和解，或者联合起来共同反抗英国的殖民统治并宣布独立。

1776 年 1 月 9 日，潘恩匿名发表了他的《常识》，大声疾呼美国必须独立。他分析了美国独立的可行性、抨击了英国的君主制对殖民地的种种恶行，号召建立美国海军力量，建议成立美国政府并提出了一系列设想。《常识》发表后立即引起轰动，鼓舞了殖民地人民争取独立的决心，指明了殖民地人民斗争的目标。在三个月内，《常识》印刷了 25 次，发行了 12 万册[38]（一说销售达 50 万册）。1776 年 2 月 14 日，潘恩为《常识》第三版写了引言和后

---

[38] ［美］詹姆斯·柯比等著，范道丰等译：《美国史》上册，商务印书馆 2012 年版，第 197 页。

记，进一步阐述了他的主张，驳斥了英国国王乔治三世反对美国独立的演讲。

也许是《常识》起了巨大作用，也许是当时形势发展的需要，也许是历史发展的必然，美国独立的形势发展与潘恩在《常识》所主张的非常一致。1776年7月4日，第二届大陆会议在费城通过了杰斐逊起草的《独立宣言》。《独立宣言》的许多内容与《常识》的观念高度一致。《宣言》阐明，一切人生而平等，具有追求幸福与自由的天赋权利，淋漓尽致地历数了英国国王在美洲大陆犯下的罪行，最后庄严宣告美利坚合众国脱离英国而独立。《独立宣言》是具有世界历史意义的伟大文献，通过《独立宣言》的这一天也成为美国脱离英国而取得独立的节日。

三、《常识》的主要内容和特点

美国独立前夕，潘恩发表了《常识》，公开提出美国独立革命的问题，并竭力强调革命之后建立共和政体才是该书的宗旨所在。它是潘恩最广为人知的一本书。第一版内容包括四个部分，到第三版时增加了后记，共五个部分：

1. 论政府的起源和目的
2. 论君主政体和世袭制度
3. 北美形势分析
4. 论北美的能力（美国独立可行性分析）

5. 后记

这本书内容很短，只有四万多字，实际上是一本宣传手册。在这本书中，潘恩的主要目的是鼓吹美国独立，并提出若干理由，其中他对英国的君主世袭制度进行了猛烈抨击，他认为这些理由是人们的常识，包括："权力长期被滥用导致对权力本身的正当性产生怀疑"；"社会是由我们的需求所产生的，而政府是由我们的罪恶所产生的"；"国王在没有被监督的情况下不可信任，或者说对绝对权力的渴望是君主制天然的弊病"；"君主制的邪恶还应该算上世袭制度，首先它扣减我们的权利，使我们变得弱小，其次把世袭当作正当的权力是对我们的侮辱和不公平"；"所有的人生而平等，任何人都不能因为出身将自己的家庭永远置于他人之上"。

潘恩的这些观念明显受到文艺复兴时期思想家们特别是同时代的欧洲的一些思想家们的影响。英国哲学家洛克[39]在其著作《政府论》中主张政府只有在取得被统治者的同意，并且保障人民拥有生命、自由和财产的自然权利时，

---

〔39〕 约翰·洛克（John Locke，1632 年 8 月 29 日～1704 年 10 月 28 日）是英国哲学家。在知识论上，洛克与乔治·贝克莱、大卫·休谟三人被列为英国经验主义（British Empiricism）的代表人物，但他也在社会契约理论上做出重要贡献。1689 年到 1690 年写成的两篇《政府论》是洛克最重要的政治论文。洛克的思想对于后代政治哲学的发展产生巨大影响，并且被广泛视为是启蒙时代最具影响力的思想家和自由主义者。他的著作也大为影响了伏尔泰和卢梭，以及许多苏格兰启蒙运动的思想家和美国开国元勋。他的理论被反映在美国的独立宣言上。

其统治才有正当性。洛克相信只有在取得被统治者的同意时，社会契约才会成立，如果缺乏了这种同意，那么人民便有推翻政府的权利。1748 年孟德斯鸠〔40〕出版《论法的精神》，全面分析了三权分立的原则。孟德斯鸠虽为贵族，他却是法国首位公开批评封建统治的思想家，他突破"君权神授"的观点，认为人民应享有宗教和政治自由；认为决定法的精神和法的内容是每个国家至关重要的；保证法治的手段是"三权分立"，即立法权、行政权和司法权分属于三个不同的国家机关，三者相互制约、权力均衡。伏尔泰〔41〕深刻剖析了君主专断的种种弊端，认识到"君主使人感到枷锁的分量"，主张以法治国，反对君主专断。他断言，人只有在自己的人格与自由得到尊重与保障的前提下，才能发挥自己的理性，推动社会繁荣。卢梭〔42〕提出"天赋人权说"，反对专制、暴政。他认为人与人的契

---

〔40〕 夏尔·德·塞孔达·孟德斯鸠男爵（法语：Charles de Secondat, Baron de Montesquieu，1689 年 1 月 18 日 ~ 1755 年 2 月 10 日），法国启蒙时期思想家、律师，也是西方国家学说和法学理论的奠基人。

〔41〕 伏尔泰，本名弗朗索瓦 - 马利·阿鲁埃（François - Marie Arouet）（1694 ~ 1778 年），伏尔泰是他的笔名。法国启蒙思想家、文学家、哲学家、史学家。伏尔泰是 18 世纪法国资产阶级启蒙运动的旗手，被誉为"法兰西思想之王""法兰西最优秀的诗人""欧洲的良心"。主张开明的君主政治，强调自由和平等。代表作《哲学通信》《形而上学论》《路易十四时代》《老实人》等。

〔42〕 让 - 雅克·卢梭（Jean - Jacques Rousseau，1712 年 6 月 28 日 ~ 1778 年 7 月 2 日），法国 18 世纪伟大的启蒙思想家、哲学家、教育家、文学家，18 世纪法国大革命的思想先驱，杰出的民主政论家和浪漫主义文学流派的开创者，启蒙运动最卓越的代表人物之一。主要著作有《论人类不平等的起源和基础》《社会契约论》《爱弥儿》《忏悔录》《新爱洛漪丝》《植物学通信》等。

约构成社会，人与社会的契约构成国家。以上这些思想家们对于君主制的批判，对于社会组成的学说在《常识》中都有反映。潘恩以他雄辩和质朴的语言将这个问题阐述的更加简明和易懂，他说："政府的起源和发展是源自于道德治理的不足而产生的一种治理模式，这也是政府的建立和目的所在，即为了人们的自由和安全。尽管表象可能模糊我们的眼睛，声音可能欺骗我们的耳朵，偏见可能蒙蔽我们的智慧，利益可能阻碍我们的理解，但是自然和理性简明的呼唤告诉我们政府之建立目的理应如此。"

潘恩风格质朴和犀利的言语与他的背景有关。他出身贫苦，早年为生计而做过许多工作，没有受过高等教育。这些经历也影响了他的文风。他的《常识》等文章言辞犀利、态度鲜明，没有学究气息。这些特点可能也适合当时美洲殖民地人们的喜爱，在斗争中起到鼓舞人心的作用。从《常识》内容中可以看出潘恩的性格比较激进，充满了斗争精神，但他有些语言也说得比较绝对，例如，他在《常识》第三版的后记中对英国国王乔治三世进行了猛烈攻击，他说："国王们不懂天理，天理也不容国王。虽然国王们的存在是由于我们的创造，但是他们不懂我们，反而成为高居创造者们之上的神。国王演讲并没有蓄意欺骗。当然即使他想骗，我们也会不受其欺骗。他把野蛮和独裁写在脸上，他使我们明白无误：每一行每次读来都使我们坚信，在丛林中裸身打猎、尚未开化的印第安人都没有英国国王残暴。"继而，他对于普通民众也提出了一些要求，宣称："不管出于任何机动，对低级和邪恶的表演表现哪怕一点点赞同的迎合甚至沉默都是有害的。"他还对拥护国王的观念的进行了猛烈批判，认为这"是明目张胆的偶像崇拜。任何人听了这种论调如果能平静地接受，就丧失了对理性追求，自甘不齿于人类，这种人应当被认为不仅放弃了做人的尊严，畜牲不如，只是像蛆虫一样在地上卑贱地爬行。"这些文辞已经超出了正常讨论问题的程度，成为强烈的责骂，对象也扩大到不特定的普通民众。

潘恩是主张自由的，是反对专制独裁的。自由就应当允许人们有不同观点，宽容人们有不同的态度和立场，不能要求所有的人都赞同自己的观念，不宜对不同观念进行言语上的责骂，甚至压制。潘恩以及他同时代的法国大革命中的一些激进人士，如罗伯斯庇尔、马拉等人都表现了对不同意见不容忍的倾向。这些主张自由和人权的人们的一些言行却违背了自己的主张，这种状况造成了许多悲剧。潘恩本人后来的遭遇也是一场悲剧，他因为与罗伯斯庇尔等人意见不合被关进监狱，几乎丧命；他后来也对美国政府和华盛顿表示不满，特别是他对宗教的攻击使他成为众矢之的，最后凄然离世。当然，潘恩后来的悲剧结局并不能减弱潘恩《常识》的历史作用和文章魅力。

一个人一生会经历各种事情，很难没有遗憾和错误；而且一件事情，一种观念的对错也非常难说，有些事情需要经过历史的检验才能知道对错，甚至过了若干时间以后仍然难下定论。潘恩的《常识》已经发表 240 年。书中关于美国独立的主张和对美国独立的许多设想在美国独立和建国的进程中早已被实现了。240 年后重读这本书，对于我们了解那段历史，了解当时的想法还是有所帮助的。如果直接阅读英文原文对于学习英语也有一定帮助。

四、《常识》的中文本

潘恩《常识》的中文本较多，笔者所知的有十几个不同的译者和不同出版社的版本，按出版时间排列如下：

1. 《常识》载《潘恩选集》，马清槐译，商务印书馆 1981 年版。

2. 《常识》，何实译，华夏出版社 2004 年版。

3. 《常识、理性时代》（潘恩两本著作合集英文注释版），支顺福译，上海外语教育出版社 2006 年版。

4. 《常识》，曾尔恕、王铮译，陕西人民出版社 2011 年版。

5. 《常识》，张源译，译林出版社 2012 年版。

6. 《常识》（英汉对照），田素雷、常凤艳译，中国对外翻译出版公司 2012 年版。

7. 《常识》（中英文双语），李玉冰译，哈尔滨出版社 2012 年版。

8.《常识（中英双语彩插本）》，余瑾译，中华书局 2013 年版。

9.《常识》（英汉双语对照），李芳华译，中国青年出版社 2013 年版。

10.《常识》，马万利译，译林出版社 2015 年版。

11.《常识》（经典珍藏大字版），韩禹译，石油工业出版社 2015 年版。

12.《常识》（改变美国的 20 本书），蒋漫译，上海译文出版社 2015 年版。

13.《常识》，周喜峰、李静宇译，民主与建设出版社 2015 年版。

14.《常识》，赵田园译，北京大学出版社 2015 年版。

15.《常识》（权威全译本），马清槐译，商务印书馆 2015 年版。

以上这些译者为我国广大读者阅读和了解《常识》做了很大贡献，其中马清槐先生的译本两次出版，第一次是由商务印书馆于 1981 年在《潘恩选集》中全文收录，第二次于 2015 年出了单行本。马清槐先生是我国翻译界的老前辈，曾担任国家出版总署编译局秘书，人民出版社编辑，时代出版社编辑，高等教育出版社编辑组长，商务印书馆编辑组长，中国翻译工作者协会第一届理事。他翻译的《常识》时间早、影响大，商务印书馆在其翻译的《常识》单行本上注明（权威全译本）字样是当之无愧的。

曾尔恕、王铮翻译《常识》译本质量很高。曾老师是我的前辈同事，长期担任中国政法大学图书馆馆长和博士生导师，外语和法律都有很深造诣。该书由潘汉典审校。在我收集的所有《常识》译本中唯有此译本标明审校者，可见此译本之认真和独特。潘汉典老先生是我景仰的前辈，他于 1948 年毕业于东吴大学比较法研究所，获法学硕士学位，是中国政法大学比较法研究所创建人、原所长；著名法学家、法学翻译家。读此译本，从字里行间可以看出译者和审校者精心翻译的印迹，我在阅读和翻译过程中，从该译本中学习和参考最多。

马万利的译本质量也非常好。据该书译者简介中介绍，马万利是历史学博士，曾在美国宾夕法尼亚大学"麦克尼尔早期美国研究中心"访问学者、合作研究员，现任大连理工大学教授、博士生导师。马万利的译本非常认真，我多次认真阅读该译本，收获和启发良多。

鉴于篇幅关系，我不能对每个译者和译本加以介绍。在此谨对每位译者表示感谢。

一本二百年前外国人写的小册子，在短时间内出现这么多中文译本，每个译者和译本各有特点，比较阅读，深受启发。既然有这么多译本，我们为什么要花近一年的时间重新翻译出版此书，有无必要这样做？我以为还是有必要的。我们这本《常识译注》（以下简称"拙译"）与我所知的译本有所不同，主要在以下几个方面：

第一，拙译对《常识》的作者和写作背景进行了较详细的介绍，对书中提及的各个人物、事件进行了注解。这可能对我国读者阅读和了解该书的有关背景有所帮助。

第二，拙译对《常识》许多表述的理解与其他译者不一样，例如：

例句 1：In the following sheets, the author hath studiously avoided every thing which is personal among ourselves. Compliments as well as censure to individuals make no part thereof. The wise, and the worthy, need not the triumph of a pamphlet; and those whose sentiments are injudicious, or unfriendly, will cease of themselves unless too much pains are bestowed upon their conversion. 这是《常识》第三版引言中的一段话。各种译本差异很大：

有人译为："在下面的文章中，笔者将有意避免谈论我们中间的任何人。这里绝无对个人的恭维或者苛责。圣贤之人不必靠小册子取胜；而那些见识浅薄之辈，或心怀敌意之徒，只要转变的过程不是太痛苦，也自会偃旗息鼓。"

也有人译为："在下文的论述中，作者谨慎地回避了任何涉及我们个人感情因素的地方，文中也没有对任何个人的赞美或指责。明智者和值得赞美之人是不需要利用这本小册子的成功来扬名天下的；而那些不明智或不要友好的人也终将转变态度、停止攻讦，只是我们要花费很大力气罢了。"

还有人译为："作者在下文中刻意回避了所有个人化的东西；因此，本书没有对任何个人加以赞美或抨击。睿智杰出之人无需凭借一册书而成名，浅薄敌对之人终会自善其身，除非转变会给他们带来无法承受的磨难。"

笔者认为：这句话其实是作者自谦之说，意为他的这本小书（指《常识》），无论对明智的人和固执的人都将不会起到太大的作用，其含义是："在下文中，作者谨慎的避免牵涉到个人的情感，不对任何个人提出赞美和批评。因为明智的人们不需要一本小手册激励；而偏见固执的人们，仍将无所作为，除非太多的痛苦迫使他们转变。"

例句 2： It hath been reported of the late Mr Pelham (who tho' an able minister was not without his faults) that on his being attacked in the house of commons, on the score, that his measures were only of a temporary kind, replied, "they will last my time." Should a thought so fatal and unmanly possess the colonies in the present contest, the name of ancestors will be remembered by future generations with detestation. 该段之中 "they will last my time." 这一句各译家差异较大。

有人译为："它们在我活着的时候总可以推行。"
也有人译为："它们会延长我的时间。"
还有人译为："这些政策在我有生之年持续执行。"

　　笔者以为，此句结合上下文理解，其意为："它们在我的任期得以实行就行了。"（我之后就管不了啦）。因为英国首相不同于国王，首相有任期的限制，他只能说某些措施在其任期内得以执行，而首相卸任之后就不可再干预政事了。

　　例句3：The Terrible privateer, Captain Death, stood the hottest engagement of any ship last war, yet had not twenty sailors on board, though her complement of men was upwards of two hundred.

　　有人译为："在上一次战争中，那艘'坚不可摧'的'死神船长号'武装民船在最激烈的海战中坚持了下来，船中共有逾二百人，而海员却不足二十人。"

　　也有人译为："那艘'恐怖的'武装民船'死亡船长'，同任何船只都做过最激烈的交战，船上的水手都不足二十人，虽然编制中的人数可高达二百人以上。"

　　还有人译为："那艘'可怖的'武装民船'死神船长'，在上次战争中同任何船只作了最激烈的战斗，但是船上的水兵不到二十人，虽然编制中的人数在二百人以上。"

　　笔者认为此句的含义是：那艘"恐怖号私掠船"在"死亡船长"的指挥下经历了最激烈战斗。在最后的一场战斗中当时船上能坚守岗位者已不足20名人员，而操纵该船的管理人员和水手实际配制为200人。

　　笔者列举以上差异并不意指以上译者谁对谁错，更不

敢保证我们是对的。不同的译者对原文理解不一样和中文
表述不一样是很正常的事情，阅读不同风格的翻译作品对
读者而言是加深对原著理解的好机会。还有些差异是由于
译者所采用的不同的英语版本中的差异造成的。例如《常
识》英文第三版的影印本中有一句：

And however our eyes may be dazzled with show, or our ears deceived by sound; however prejudice may warp our wills, or interest
darken our understanding, the simple voice of nature and of reason
will say, it is right.

有人译为："不管漫天冰雪使我们如何眼花缭乱，我们
的耳朵如何难辩声音真假，也不管偏见如何歪曲我们的意
志，或者个人的利害如何困扰我们的理解，自然和理性质
朴的声音毕竟会说这种方式是对的。"

笔者译为："尽管表象可能模糊我们的眼睛，声音可
能欺骗我们的耳朵，偏见可能蒙蔽我们的智慧，利益可能
阻碍我们的理解，但是自然和理性简明的呼唤告诉我们政
府之建立目的理应如此。"产生这种差异的原因在于有些
《常识》的英文版中"show"这个词写作"snow"，从而产
生了中文翻译的差异。

第三，一本二百多年前写成的英文小册子，现在有若
干中文译本，说明这本书在中国有不少读者，他们或者对
美国独立前的这段历史感兴趣，或者对《常识》这本书中

所包含的知识感兴趣，或者对语言和翻译感兴趣，不管人们对《常识》的兴趣何在，阅读这本书总能增加一些对历史的了解。

由于《常识》是二百多年前的英文作品，又由于《常识》中包含了大量的历史典故、当时的人物、事件，对一些中国读者可能有些困难。也许在中国直接读《常识》英文原版的人并不很多，以上这些《常识》的中文本对普及《常识》有很大作用，但是，一些中译本中费解的句子，各中译本中存在的差异，以及文章中的典故都可能影响中文版的阅读和理解。

我刚开始阅读《常识》英文版时也觉得吃力，坚持阅读、对每一句反复琢磨，对其中涉的每一个典故、每一个事件反复查询，渐渐就懂了。每当搞清楚一句甚至一个词的真实含意，心中的喜悦难以言表。我翻译《常识》完全是偶然的、业余的。所谓偶然是我原来没有翻译此书的计划，偶然读到这本书，偶然对其语言和内容很感兴趣，偶然发现有许多中文本，偶然发现中文本之间有差异，偶然发现我对《常识》的英文本中一些意思的理解与现在的中文本有些不同，所以就把我的理解以及相关的背景知识以注解的方式记录了下来。所谓业余指我不是英语专业的，也不是历史专业的，也不是专职翻译，只是对翻译感兴趣而已。由于水平问题，我在翻译过程中遇到不少困难。幸好有《常识》以前的中文译本作参考，才得以完成这项工作，特别是曾尔恕教授等人翻译并经潘汉典教授审校的译本（陕西人民出版社 2011 年版）、马万利的译本（译林出版社 2015 年版）和马清槐的译本（商务印书馆出1981 年版）。在译注《常识》过程中，我仔细阅读了前人的这些译本并与原著进行了逐字的对照，受到很大启发，为此，我谨向各位译者表示感谢。翻译不容易，翻译名著更不容易，翻译二百多年前的名著尤其不容易。为此，我对《常识》的各个中文版译者表示钦佩。

我的专业是法律，学习和研究中外法律数十年，这本书中许多与法律问题相关的论述对我而言比较容易；另外我也曾经在美国耶鲁大学和英国伦敦大学等学校学习过一段时间，访问过书中提到的各个国家，包括英国、美国、法国、西班牙、以色列、土耳其、俄罗斯等，对书中提到的地方和曾经发生的历史事件也有一定了解。这些对我翻译此书也有一定帮助。尽管如此，我仍然觉得翻译此书没有把握。幸好内子是学英语的，毕业于上海外国语大学，长期从事英语教学工作，也曾在英国和美国学习，她慨然愿意与我一起承担这项翻译工作。于是，我们二人合作才完成了这本小书的翻译。

《常识》的中文本有不少，英文本也有不少，有些中译本后附有英文本。我翻译时采用的英文原文版本是 1776年《常识》第三版影印本，由美国 SIGNET CLASSICS 印书馆于 2003 年出版。由于影印不太清楚，本书所附的《常识》英文本来自网络 Word 版本，并以影印本为准进行了校对，特此说明。

我在本书附录中还附上了《英国国王乔治三世对议会的演说》和《美国独立宣言》的中英文本。附上英国国王演讲的理由是：潘恩在《常识》中，特别是在《常识》的第三版后记中对英国国王乔治三世进行了猛烈抨击，对"国王的演讲"进行了强烈的驳斥。为了使读者了解英国国王说了些什么而成为潘恩批判的靶子，有必要附上原文。国王的演讲原文是英文，中文是我自己译的。附上《美国独立宣言》的理由是：该宣言中有许多内容反映了潘恩的思想。我不敢肯定《独立宣言》的起草人杰斐逊的观念来自潘恩，但他们二人皆为美国独立作出了重大贡献。《常识》和《美国独立宣言》的观念一致，甚至某些表述一致，但这并不说明是谁抄袭了谁的观念，而是作者们对真理的一致认识使然，这两个文件都对美国独立起到巨大作用。《美国独立宣言》中文有若干版本，各中文版本之间及与英文原文之间有不少不一致的表述。因为年代已久，每个中文版本译者为谁已不可考。我所用的《独立宣言》的英文本出自董云虎编著的《人权基本文献要览》[43]，我重新翻译《独立宣言》时参考了该书中《独立宣言》的中文版和网上流行的一些中文版，谨向这些未知名的译者

---

〔43〕 董云虎编著：《人权基本文献要览》，辽宁人民出版社 1994 年版，第 16～22 页。

表示感谢。

我们对《常识》原文的理解与我所读过的中文本有一定差异，我不敢肯定我们的理解是正确的，更不敢说别人翻译有错误，我只能保证我们认真地琢磨了原文的每一句话，尽我们所能将我们理解的意思用中文转述出来。为了读懂《常识》，我在翻译的过程中将内容中涉及的每一人、每一事件、每一历史典故、每一处引用都进行了核对并记下了出处，并以译者注的形式加在《常识》的相关之处。所以在《常识译注》中除了特别说明的之外，所有的脚注都是译者所加，供有兴趣的读者参考。希望我们所加的这些注解不致增加读者的负担，如果有读者认为注解多余，请忽略其存在；如果有读者发现我们注解中有错误，请向我们指出。

近年来中国有十几家出版社分别出版了潘恩的《常识》中译本。我们认为，该书内容包含许多法律知识，作为政法类书籍出版更为合适，所以希望这本《常识译注》由中国政法大学出版社出版，承蒙该社应允，我们十分感谢。我自 1979 年来到中国政法大学读书，至今已经 37 年。中国政法大学给了我知识和工作，对我恩重如山。内子自 1983 年来中国政法大学工作，至今也有 33 年。中国政法大学就是我们的家。我们把这本书作为交给母校的一份作业。该书交稿之后，出版社的编辑对全书的中英文内容都进行了极其认真的检查和校对，提出了许多宝贵的修改意见，令我们很感动和感激。值此书付印之际，请允许我们向此书的编辑李云琦女士表示衷心感谢，向所有帮助该书出版的同仁们表示衷心感谢，向我的母校中国政法大学表示衷心感谢。

潘恩的《常识》已经问世二百多年，由于我们的水平有限，对当年的历史、书中所涉及的人物和事件以及对当年的语言风格知之甚少，我们的错误在所难免，敬请读者诸君指正。

杨宇冠

2016 年 1 月 9 日第一稿

2016 年 1 月 29 日第二稿

2016 年 3 月 19 日第三稿

2016 年 7 月 19 日定稿

常　识

托马斯·潘恩

引　言

下文中所包含的观点可能不够流行，不足以得到普遍赞同。人们习惯于长期不思考某件事的荒谬，以致使它表面上看来正确，而且会首先大声疾呼以维护这种习惯。但是，这种混乱很快就会平息，因为时间比理性更具有转变力量。

权力长期被滥用导致对权力本身的正当性产生怀疑（但是如果受害者没有被激怒到对此事产生怀疑的程度，这种现象可能从未被人们想起）。英格兰国王使用"他自己的权力"支持他称之为"他们的议会"。当这片土地上善良的人民悲惨地受制于双重压迫时，他们有无可争辩的权利，质疑国王和议会的权力，并且可以拒绝他们的掠夺。

在下文中，作者谨慎地避免牵涉到个人的情感，不对任何个人提出赞美和批评。因为明智的人们不需要一本小手册激励；而偏见固执的人们，将仍然无所作为，除非太多的痛苦迫使他们转变。[44]

美利坚[45]的事业在很大程度上是全人类的事业，许

---

　　〔44〕　这句话是作者自谦之说，意为他的这本小书（指《常识》），对明智的人和固执的人都将不会起到太大的作用。

　　〔45〕　原文为"America"，指欧洲人新发现的美洲大陆，包括北美洲和南美洲。在本书写作时，美国还没有独立，作者在此书中使用"美利坚"一词指英国在北美的13个殖民地的总称。"美利坚"一词来自亚美利哥·韦斯普奇（意

多事件已经发生和将要发生，这些事件的影响并非局限于本地区，而且有全局性意义。通过这些事件，对人类怀有爱心之人的原则将会受到影响，这些事件也与他们的情感有关。用火和剑使这片土地荒芜，向全人类的自然权力宣战，将维护自己权利的人赶尽杀绝，这些恶行关系到每一个人，不分阶级和党派，因为自然赋予了人们思考的能力，本书作者是这些人们中的一员。

又及，本书新版已经拖延，是为了（如果必要的话）了解反驳独立原则的任何企图，到目前为止还没有回应出现。鉴于公众了解这种行为并作出此种举动所需的时间已经过去，所以假定今后也没有。本书作者是谁，这对于公

_____

（接上页）大利文：Amerigo Vespucci，1454 年 3 月 9 日～1512 年 2 月 22 日）。他是意大利的商人、航海家、探险家和旅行家，1497 年，亚美利哥从欧洲前往美洲。当时"新大陆"还没有一个总括大陆的名称。在当时所有的人包括哥伦布在内都认为这块大陆是亚洲东部。亚美利哥经过对南美洲海岸的考察提出这是一块新大陆。德国地理学家马丁·瓦尔德泽米勒（Martin Waldseemüller，约 1470 年～1520 年 3 月 16 日）得知消息后，提议新大陆采用"亚美利加"作为名字，即采用拉丁语 Amerious 深化为 Americ，并加指地后缀－a，构成了 America，意为"亚美利哥·韦斯普奇发现的土地"。这个地名就此定了下来，全称亚美利加洲。18 世纪前，英国在北美大西洋沿岸陆续建立了 13 个殖民地，当时称为北美 13 州联合殖民地。1775 年这些殖民地人民发动了反对英国殖民统治的独立战争，1776 年 7 月 4 日，殖民地人民发表了独立宣言，宣布成立美利坚合众国，并把美洲的名称作为自己的名称。1787 年在美国宪法中正式肯定了这一名称。美利坚合众国（The United States of America）简称美国（U. S. A.）。在英语中，亚美利加和美利坚为同一词"America"，只是汉译不同，前者指全美洲，后者指美国。美国各州（State）也只是在美国独立之后的称呼。因为"State"这个词有国家的意思，所以美国全称为"美利坚合众国"，直译为"美利坚各国联合体"。

众而言微不足道，值得注意的是原则本身而不是个人。然而，不可不说的是他不属于任何党派，能够影响作者的只是理性和原则，而不是任何公众和个人。

1776 年 2 月 14 日于费城

论政府的起源和目的，兼评英国政体

一些作者[46]混淆社会和政府的概念，以便使得它们很少区别，甚至完全没有区别。然而，它们不仅有区别而且有不同的起源。社会是由我们的需求所产生的，而政府是因我们的罪恶所产生的。前者从正面以凝聚我们爱心的方式促进我们的幸福，后者从反面以限制我们邪恶的方式保障我们的幸福。一个促进人们的交流，另一个制造人们的差别。第一个是保护者，第二个是惩罚者。

社会在任何状态下都是有益的，而政府在其最好的状态下也是不可避免的罪恶，在其最坏的情况下是难以忍受的恶魔。当我们遭受苦难，或者面临在无政府的地方才有的那种苦难时，我们可能期望这片土地没有政府；每当想起我们的苦难是由我们自己所供养的政府带来的，我们的悲哀更加使人痛心。政府如衣服，是失去纯真的标志。国王们的宫殿都是建立在天堂的废墟之上。如果一个人的良知的搏动是清晰的、持久如一的和不可抗拒的，他将不需要任何立法者。但是事实并非如此，他发现需要放弃他的

---

〔46〕 原文为"writers"，潘恩写出书时正值18世纪思想启蒙时代，许多人撰写和发表书籍文章探讨社会问题。潘恩此处没有注明下文引用的是何具体人的观点，只是泛指。鉴于"作家"一词在中文语境下常指撰写文学类作品的人，所以此处译为"作者"更妥当。

部分财产供养政府以保护他的其他财产。在这种情况下，他会根据以往做事的经验，怀着谨慎的态度两害取其轻。设计政府的真正意图和目的应当是安全，所以毋庸置疑的结论是，不论政府的形式如何，它应该显示出能够为我们提供最大的保护，即代价最小且福利最大的政府才是大家所希望的。

为了对设置政府的目的和意图有清晰和公正的理解，我们设想一小群人在一个与世隔绝的地方居住，与世界其他地方隔绝联系，他们代表任何国家或这个世界上的第一批移民。在这种自然的自由情况下，他们首先想到的是社会，许多动机促使他们这样做。一个人的力量与他的需求是不匹配的，他的精神不适宜永久的孤单。所以他将很快不得不寻求其他人的帮助和慰藉，而其他人也有同样的需求。四五个人联合起来可以在旷野之中建立起一个简易的住所，但是一个人劳苦一生也可能一事无成。当他砍倒一棵大树时，他不能移动这棵树，即使移动了，也不可能竖起来，同时饥饿将驱使他停止劳作，各种不同的需求，以不同方式对他形成各种困扰。疾病或者不幸可能导致死亡，虽然这些可能都不是致命的，但是都可以让他难以存活，使其陷入生不如死的境地。

如此，需求如同吸引力一样很快就会使先民们形成社会，因为相互扶持至关重要。如果他们能够保持公正地对待彼此这种好关系，法律责任和政府都没有存在必要。然而只有天堂才能没有邪恶，人世间不可避免的事情终将发生，即当先民们团结起来克服了起初的困难之后，他们便开始松懈了自己的责任和与别人彼此依赖的联系。这种缺陷表明人们有必要建立某种形式的政府以补充道德的缺陷。

一棵合适的大树可能成为移民们的会场，全体移民聚集在树干之下讨论公共事务。他们的第一部法律极有可能是管理规则，执行该规则的手段只是对违反者加以鄙视作为惩罚。在这个原始议会之中，每一个人根据他们的自然权利都有一个席位。[47]

起初，定居者人数很少，距离临近，公众事务简单。随着定居地的增加，公众关心的事项也相应增加，居住地距离遥远使他们在某一时段同时开会极为不便。这些变化使他们觉得有必要同意将立法事务交由从全体民众中选出的部分代表管理，这些人所关心的事项应当与推举他们的人保持一致。如果移民继续增加，则有必要增加代表的数量，这样移民地中每一部分的利益都将得到关注，人们发现最好将移民们的定居地划分成若干适宜的部分，每一个部分派出自己适当的代表，被选出的代表不能形成与选民们不同的利益。出于谨慎的考虑，选举应当经常举行，因

---

〔47〕 潘恩描述的这种现象并非出于其想象，历史上曾经发生。本书译者曾经参观过冰岛议会旧址国家公园（Thingvellir），有"世界最古老的民主议会会址"之称。公元930年，经39个定居酋长倡议，在此会址召开名为阿耳庭（Althingi）的全体居民大会，并由此而得名。该地依山傍湖，有天然的讲台和会场，据说与会者对所议之事都有发言权和表决权。

为这样被选的代表才能在几个月内回到和融入广大选民中间。为了防止被公众追责，代表必须保证对公众的忠诚。这种经常的交流将与社会的每一个部分建立起共同的利益，他们将自然的互相支持，政府的力量和被统治的人们的幸福皆有赖于这种机制（而不是那种毫无意义的帝王的名号）。

这就是政府的起源和发展的根源。它源自于道德治理的不足而产生的一种治理模式，这也是政府建立的目的所在，即为了人们的自由和安全。尽管表象可能模糊我们的眼睛，声音可能欺骗我们的耳朵，偏见可能蒙蔽我们的智慧，利益可能阻碍我们的理解，但是自然和理性简明的呼唤告诉我们政府之建立目的理应如此。

我关于政府的观点来自于自然法则，这是任何人力不能够推翻的，即越简单的事情越不会发生混乱，即使混乱了，也更容易改正。从这个角度出发，我对备受吹捧的英国政体提出一些评论。我承认，在黑暗和奴役时代建立起来的英国政体是高尚的。当世界专制横行时，对专制的任何一点改动都是对人民的伟大的解救[48]。但显而易见的

---

〔48〕　潘恩此处可能指英国的"光荣革命"（Glorious Revolution）。1688 年，英国资产阶级和新贵族发动的推翻詹姆斯二世的统治，防止天主教复辟的非暴力政变。这场革命未有流血，因此历史学家将其称之为"光荣革命"。1689 年英国议会通过了限制王权的《权利法案》（The Bill of Rights），全称《国民权利与自由和王位继承宣言》（An Act Declaring the Rights and Liberties of the Subject and Settling the Succession of the Crown）。英国的君主立宪制政体即起源于这次光

是，当下英国的政体还是不完美的，是容易被颠覆的，是难以兑现其承诺的。

绝对的专制（虽然是人性的耻辱）也有一定的优势，它们直截了当。在这种情况下，人民遭受痛苦可以知道苦难的根源出自谁的脑袋，并且知道补救的方式，不会被各种措施和救助所迷惑。但是英国政体是如此复杂，国民们长年累月受苦受难而不能发现问题所在。不同的人提出不同的问题，每一个政治医生开出不同的药方。

我深知克服地方的或长期存在的偏见是困难的，但是如果我们认真的审视英国政体的各个部分，我们会发现，它们是两种古代专制卑劣的残余与一些新的共和因素的混合体。

第一，国王是君主专制的残余。

第二，上议院人员是贵族统治的残余。

第三，新的共和因素存在于下议院的人员之中，他们的作用决定了英国的自由。[49]

（接上页）荣革命。《权利法案》内容只有十三条，主要有：凡未经议会同意，以国王权威停止法律或停止法律实施之僭越权力，为非法权力；凡未经议会准许，国王利用特权征收，或供国王使用而征收金钱，超出国会准许之时限或方式者，皆为非法；向国王请愿，乃臣民之权利，一切对此项请愿之判罪或控告，皆为非法；议会之选举应是自由的；不应要求过多的保释金，亦不应强课过分之罚款，更不应滥施残酷非常之刑罚；为申雪一切诉冤，并为修正、加强与维护法律起见，国会应时常集会。

〔49〕 在此潘恩论述了英国政体的三个主要的组成部分，即英国国王和英国议会（The Parliament of United Kingdom）。英国议会为两院制，由上议院和下议院共同组成。上院（House of Lords）又称"贵族院"，下院（House of Commons）又称"平民院"。英国议会创建于13世纪，迄今已有700多年的历史，

前两种之产生源于世袭继承，不取决于人民。因此，他们在宪政的角度对国家的自由毫无贡献。

宣称英国的政体是三种权力相互制约的体制，是荒谬的，这些话语毫无意义，或者它们显然不能自圆其说。

宣称下院是对国王的制约隐含着两层意思。

第一，国王在没有被监督的情况下不可信任，或者说对绝对权力的渴望是君主制天然的弊病。

第二，下院的议员们被指派上述任务，意味着他们比国王更聪明或者更值得信赖。

同一个宪政体制给予下院权力以控制国王供给的方式制约国王，但是随后又给国王以否决下院法案的权力来制约下院。本来下院议员被推定为比国王更贤明，但是从这个机制可推论出国王比这些人更贤明。这真是荒谬绝伦。

在君主制的组成中有一些特别愚蠢的事情，首先它阻止了一个人得到信息的渠道，然后又授权他在需要做出最高级的判断的时候采取行动的权力。国王的身份使他与世

（接上页）被称为"议会之母"。上院的议员不是选举产生的，而是由王室后裔、世袭贵族、法律贵族、家权贵族、终身贵族、苏格兰贵族、爱尔兰贵族、离任首相组成，无任期限制。国王可以临时增封爵位，而议员死亡无需增补，所以贵族院议员人数不定。贵族多数是保守党人，而且老人占多数，相当于终身制，贵族院议员平均年龄为60多岁，80岁以上的也有不少人。这些贵族不拿薪金，但上一天班可拿一定的车马费。开会时议长担任主席。上院开会时间与下院相同。英国下议院是民主的代议机关。下院议员通过普选、平等、直接、秘密的方式进行选举，但贵族、主教、法官、高级文官、现役军人、宣布破产者、重罪犯人、受权办理选举事务的负责人等不能担任下议院的议员。

隔绝，然而国王的职责却要求他对外界的事务有通透的了解。这些不同的方面互相对立和破坏，证明了整个体制的荒谬和无用。

有些作者如此解释英国的政体，他们宣称：国王作为一方，人民作为另一方，上院代表国王，下院代表人民。虽然这种提法很委婉，但是把议院分割成互相对立的不同部分，如果仔细审视就能发现这种表述是既不能自圆其说，又含混不清。人们常见这种现象：用华丽辞藻形容某种不存在的或者超出了理解范围的事物，只能愉悦人们的耳朵，但不能使人理解。这种解释包含着一个前提，如果人民害怕给国王以某种权力，并且还总是被要求承担制约这种权力的责任，那么国王的这种权力是从哪里来的？明智的人民不会把这种权力作为礼物送给国王，任何需要制约的权力也都不是来自上帝的礼物。然而英国宪法〔50〕中却设想存在着这种权力。

宪法的这种规定与其任务不相称，实施的方式不能达到其目标，整体如同一种自杀式的机制。正如比较重的物体总是能带动较轻的物体，又如一个机器所有齿轮的运转是由一个齿轮驱动的，所以问题是我们必须知道英国政体的哪一种权力是最重要的，因为这种权力起到主导作用，

---

〔50〕 英国宪法并不是一个单一的书面文件，也不是一成不变的法律条文。它是由一系列涉及英国国体、政体，特别是关于国王、贵族、平民的权利等法律法规组成的。

通过其他权力或者一部分的权力互相配合，互相制约。但是如果提供制约的这些部件不能够发挥制动这台机器的作用，那么这些部件的工作都是无效的。这种机制的原动力一直发挥作用直到最后，虽然缺乏速度，但它可以一直拖延下去。

很显然，英国王权是英国政体中压倒一切的主导力量。王室之权的实现仅仅是通过授予职事和津贴而实现的。虽然我们足够聪明，关闭和锁上君主独裁制的大门，但同时我们又非常愚蠢的把大门的钥匙交给了王室。

英国人支持由国王、贵族院和平民院组成的政府统治是一种偏见。这种偏见来自于国民骄傲感而不是理性。毫无疑问，个人在英格兰要比在某些国家的人更有安全感，但是英国如同法国一样，国王的意志就是法律，所不同的是它不是直接从国王口中发出，而是以可怕的议会法案的形式对人民发号施令。查理一世的命运〔51〕只是使国王们更加阴险狡猾而不是更加公正。

所以，不论英国民族对某种模式的偏爱和偏见，英国

----

〔51〕　此处指英国国王查理一世被处死的命运。查理一世与议会不和，引发英国内战，被认定国王对人民发动战争而被审判。1649 年 1 月英国成立一个高级法庭审理查理一世，国王被带到威斯敏斯特大厅受审。由于查理一世从最开始就不承认这个法庭的合法性，因而也不为自己的行为认真辩护。27 日，135 名特别法庭成员 59 人签署了由克伦威尔下达的处死国王的命令。罪名是背叛他的国家，背叛他的人民。1649 年 1 月 30 日早晨，查理一世被执行死刑，终年 49 岁。

王室不似土耳其王室残暴[52]的原因显而易见的是因为英国人民的素质而不是英国的政体使然。

现在正是需要探讨英国政体的缺点的时候。当我们仍然处于某种主导偏见的影响之下，我们就不能以正确的态度公正地对待他人；同样，如果我们被偏见所束缚，我们就不能公正地评判自己。正如一个迷恋妓女的男人不适宜选择或评判妻子，偏爱腐朽的政体的成见使我们无法辨别什么是一个美好的制度。

---

〔52〕 土耳其（Türkiye）是一个横跨欧亚两洲的国家，北临黑海，南临地中海，东南与叙利亚、伊拉克接壤，西临爱琴海，并与希腊以及保加利亚接壤，东部与格鲁吉亚、亚美尼亚、阿塞拜疆和伊朗接壤。土耳其地理位置和地缘政治战略意义极为重要，是连接欧亚的十字路口。土耳其人是突厥人与属于欧洲人种的地中海原始居民的混血后裔。统治土耳其时间最长的奥斯曼帝国，其国王称为"苏丹"。奥斯曼一世在1299年建立奥斯曼帝国，延续到1922年才被推翻。土耳其在苏莱曼一世（1494～1566）时期达到鼎盛，统治区域地跨欧、亚、非三大洲。奥斯曼帝国的苏丹视自己为天下之主。在历史上，土耳其曾与欧洲国家发生多次战争，所以从前的一些欧洲人认为土耳其苏丹很残暴。

论君主和世袭制度

人类产生之初，所有人一律平等并无等级之分。此种平等被后来发生的一些情况所打破。且不谈人类间存在的压迫和贪婪这些难听的词语，单只是贫穷和富有的差别就在很大程度上导致了人类的不平等。压迫别人通常是富有的结果，但是压迫不是创造财富的途径；贪婪可能使一个人摆脱贫困，然而通常会使其人太胆小而不能成为富人。

但是，人与人之间还存在着另外一个重要的差别，就是把人分为国王和臣民。这种差别不能以自然的、宗教的理由所解释。男性和女性的差别是天然的，美好和丑恶的差别是由上天决定的。相比较而言，一些人来到这个世界上就得到高居其他人之上的地位，他们高贵得就像新的物种，这种现象以及这些人是创造人类幸福的救星还是造成人类悲惨的根源，这件事情值得探究。

根据《圣经》记载，在世界的远古时代没有帝王，从而也没有战争。正是因为帝王的傲慢才将人类投入混战之中。一个多世纪以来，荷兰没有国王[53]，比欧洲有王室

---

〔53〕　1579年荷兰北方省中的七省（荷兰、比利时和卢森堡的区域）成立了乌得勒支联盟，共同反对西班牙统治。1581年7月26日，来自荷兰各起义城市的代表在海牙宣布：废除西班牙国王对荷兰各省的统治权，联盟正式宣布独

的国家享受了更多和平。古代社会印证了这种观点，早期的教民们享受宁静的乡村生活，感到很幸福，但当我们阅读犹太王国的历史时，就看不见这种幸福了。

国王统治的制度首先是由异教徒发明的，以色列的子民们仿制了这种习俗。这是魔鬼为了推行偶像崇拜的最成功的发明。异教徒对他们死去的国王像神灵一样供奉，基督教世界把这种制度变本加厉，对他们活着的国王也如神灵般供奉。将"神圣的陛下"这种称号用于一个在尘世间争权夺利的凡夫俗子，这对于神圣称号是严重亵渎。

将一个凡人抬高到远远高居于众人之上的地步，违反了人类应有的平等权利，而且在经典著作中也毫无根据。正如基甸（Gideon）〔54〕和先知撒母耳（Samuel）〔55〕所宣称的那样，上帝的意旨明确反对国王统治。在君主制国家，经典中所有反对君主统治的部分都被成功地掩饰了。但是它们无疑值得那些尚未组建政府的国家重视。"凯撒的

（接上页）立，成立荷兰共和国（正式名称为尼德兰联合共和国）。1648 年西班牙国王菲利普四世才签订《明斯特条约》，承认尼德兰七省联合共和国。自那时起到潘恩写作《常识》约一百多年。

〔54〕 基甸（Gideon）是古代以色列的著名英雄和士师。据《圣经》记载：基甸率领以色列人与米甸人对阵时，以色列人只有三万二千人，而米甸人却有十三万五千人。基甸精选了数百名勇士战胜了敌人。

〔55〕 撒母耳（Samuel）是《圣经》中的人物，他是以色列最后的一位士师，也是以色列民立国后的第一位先知，他曾膏立扫罗和大卫为王。他不但是一个先知，也是祭司，更是一位伟大的军事家、政治家、宗教家。

东西归于凯撒"〔56〕这是朝庭的经典原则，但这并非君主制的根据，因为（耶稣说这句话的时候）犹太人并没有国王，还处于附属于罗马帝国的地位。

自摩西〔57〕叙述创世故事的时候直到犹太人全民被骗要求被一个国王统治，时间跨度近 3000 年。在这期间，他们治理的模式（除了特殊情况受到上帝的干预之外）是由一位士师〔58〕和部落长者联合管理的共和制度。他们没有

〔56〕　凯撒是古罗马帝国的君王，当时罗马帝国统治范围包括耶稣生活的区域。这句话的意思是："各得其所，各得其应得的。"语出《圣经·新约·马太福音书》第 22 章。那时，企图陷害耶稣的人想在言谈上叫耶稣入圈套。他们对说："夫子，我们知道你是真诚的人，按真理教授天主的道路，不顾忌任何人，因为你不看人的情面，如今请你告诉我们：给凯撒纳税，可以不可以？"耶稣看破他们的恶意，就说："假善人，你们为什么要试探我？拿一个交税的钱币给我看看！"他们便递给他一银钱。耶稣对他们说："这钱上的肖像和名号是谁的？"他们对他说："是凯撒的。"耶稣对他们说："那么，凯撒的就应归还凯撒；天主的，就应归还天主。"反对耶稣的人本来是想让耶稣为难，如果耶稣说应当向凯撒纳税则意味着他承认世俗君主的统治；如果他反对向凯撒纳税则违反了法律。

〔57〕　摩西（希伯来语：Moses）是《圣经》中的人物。天主教称为梅瑟，伊斯兰教称为穆萨，他的名字在希伯来语的意思是从水里拉上来。因为当摩西还只是一个婴儿时，埃及法老下令杀死所有犹太人的孩子。摩西的母亲只好将新出生的摩西放在篮子里然后放到河里随水漂流。在漂流过程中，法老的女儿把摩西从水里救了出来，并且为他取了名字。摩西成年之后，带领以色列人离开埃及，据《圣经》记载，在西奈山上，摩西得到了神所颁布的《十诫》，即《摩西十诫》。

〔58〕　士师这个概念出自摩西。在旷野流浪时期，他将处理一些琐碎案件的责任，交给其他人分担。这些人成了各级审判官（Judges），汉译为"士师"。《圣经·士师记》共讲述了当时 12 位高高在上的士师。人们以"大"士师和"小"士师来区分他们。"小"士师的职责就是进行狭隘意义上的审判。而"大"士师则不但要调解法律纷争，在某种程度上，他们还是具有领袖风采的

国王，在上帝的名义统治之下，尊崇任何人为国王的想法都是罪恶的。当人们反思国王被尊为偶像、受到人们狂热崇拜这种现象，他们无需怀疑，这是违反天意的，因为享有绝对尊崇和荣耀的上帝是不会赞成任何违反天意的统治形式。

君主政体在《圣经》中被列为犹太人的一种罪孽之一，因此犹太人遭受到诅咒。这段历史经验值得人们注意。

以色列的子孙被米甸人[59]压迫，基甸率领很少的军队进行抵抗，在神的帮助下取得了胜利。犹太人庆祝这次胜利，将其归功于基甸的统帅，建议立他为王，以色列人对基甸说："愿你和你的儿孙管理我们。"此处的诱惑已经达到极致，不仅是一个王国，而且是一个世袭的王国。基甸诚恳地说："我不管理你们，我的儿子也不管理你们，唯有耶和华管理你们。"[60]上文表述的非常清楚，基甸并非拒绝这份荣耀，而是否定人们给予这份荣耀的正当性。基甸并没有用客套的话语对他们表示感谢，而是本着一个

（接上页）统率。他们统治着百姓一切重要生活领域。从历史角度来计算，士师时代持续了不过150余年。《圣经》却将这段时代扩展到480年，从而精确地接架起一座连接从约书亚卒到先知撒母耳上台的时间桥梁。随着最后一名士师的死去，以色列君王时代开始了。

〔59〕 米甸人（Midianite）亦称以实马利人（Ishmaelite）。《旧约》所载与以色列人密切相关的游牧部族。其活动范围大致在阿拉伯旷野西北部亚喀巴湾以东，他们以畜牧、行商和劫掠为生。以色列人出埃及时期（西元前13世纪）和士师时期（西元前12～前11世纪）都与米甸人频繁接触。

〔60〕 译者注：见《圣经·士师记》第8章第22节。

先知的正确立场批评他们背离他们天国之主，即上帝的统治。

　　大约 130 年之后，犹太人再次犯同样的错误。他们对异教徒偶像崇拜的渴望已经达到了不可理喻的程度。在之前撒母耳的两个儿子被委托管理一些日常事务[61]，犹太人借口指责这两个儿子有一些不端行为，他们鲁莽地跑到撒母耳面前吵吵嚷嚷说："现在你已经老了，你的儿子没有走你的路。请为我们指定一个国王管理我们如同其他国家一样。"在这里，我们不得不认为他们的动机很糟糕，他们可能想效仿其他国家，即异教徒的模式，然而，他们的真正荣光与外国是完全不同的。这使撒母耳很不高兴。他向上帝祈祷，上帝告诉撒母耳说："百姓向你说的一切话，你只管依从。因为他们不是厌弃你，乃是厌弃我，不要我作他们的王。自从我领他们出埃及到如今，他们常常离弃我，事奉别神。现在他们向你所行的，是照他们素来所行的。故此你要依从他们的话，只是当警戒他们，告诉他们将来那王怎样管辖他们。"这里不是特指某个具体的国王，而是以色列人迫切想仿效的世界上国王统治模式。尽管不同的国王处于不同的时间并有不同的统治方式，他们的本质都是一样的。撒母耳将耶和华的话都传给求他立

──────────

[61]　译者注：据《圣经·撒母耳》第 8 章记载：撒母耳年纪老迈，就立他儿子作以色列的士师。长子名叫约珥，次子名叫亚比亚。他们在别是巴作士师。他儿子不行他的道，贪图财利，收受贿赂，屈枉正直。

王的百姓，说："管辖你们的王必这样行，他必派你们的儿子为他赶车，跟马，奔走在车前。（这种描述和现代压迫者的模式一样。）又派他们作千夫长，五十夫长，为他耕种田地，收割庄稼，打造军器和车上的器械。必取你们的女儿为他制造香膏，做饭烤饼。（这段描述了立王的代价和国王的奢华及压迫。）也必取你们最好的田地，葡萄园，橄榄园赐给他的臣仆。（从中我们可以看出贿赂，腐败和宠信是国王们固有的罪恶。）你们的粮食和葡萄园所出的，他必取十分之一给他的官员和臣仆。又必取你们的仆人婢女，健壮的少年人和你们的驴，供他差役。你们的羊群，他必取十分之一，你们也必作他的仆人。那时你们必因所选的王哀求耶和华，耶和华却不应允你们。"这一段解释了君主制的延续并非因为自古以来少数明君的品格，这种现象并不能使君王神圣，或者抵消了君主制开始的罪恶。人们给予大卫王的赞美并非因为他的国王身份，而是因为他作为一个凡人遵从了上帝的意志。但是，百姓竟不肯听撒母耳的话，说："不然，我们定要一个王治理我们，使我们像列国一样，有王治理我们，统领我们，为我们争战。"撒母耳继续对他们说理，批评他们负义。但是，这一切都毫无效果。看到他们如此一意孤行，撒母耳求告上帝耶和华打雷降雨（这是一种惩罚，因为当时正是麦收时候）。他要让犹太人知道而且看出：你们求立王的事是在耶和华面前犯大罪了。耶和华就在这日打雷降雨。

众人便甚惧怕耶和华和撒母耳。众人对撒母耳说，求你为仆人们祷告耶和华你的神，免得我们死亡，因为我们求立王的事正是罪上加罪了。[62] 上文引用的《圣经》内容是非常清晰肯定的，没有模棱两可的余地：上帝反对君主制的立场是真实的，或者《圣经》是虚假的。人们有正当的理由相信国王的治国之术正如神父的谋略一样，在教皇统治的国家，他们不让大家明白经文的真实意思，任何形式的君主制就如同宗教统治的政府。

君主制的邪恶之上更有甚者是世袭制度的邪恶。前者减少了我们的权利，使我们变得弱小；后者把世袭当作正当的权力，则是对我们后代的侮辱和不公。因为所有的人生而平等，任何人都不能因为出身将自己的家庭永远置于他人之上。虽然第一代国王可能有权享受一些尊敬，但是他的后代远远没有继承这些荣誉。对于国王世袭继承之荒谬最强有力的证明是，它不符合自然原理，否则它不会经常陷入荒谬的地步，即"在人类需要一头狮子的时候，上天却给了一头驴"。[63]

---

〔62〕 译者注：《圣经·撒母耳记》第 12 章第 17～19 节。

〔63〕 译者注：参见《伊索寓言·披着狮子皮的驴子》，故事梗概为："有头驴子披着狮子皮四处游荡，吓唬那些弱小无知的动物。他看见了狐狸，也想去吓唬吓唬他。狐狸正巧以前就听到过他的叫声，便对驴子说'如果我听不出你的叫声，我也会害怕了。'这是说，有些人看起来神气十足，一表人才，然而一开口就原形毕露了。"作者引用这则寓言的意思是指后代国王通过继承取得王位虽然如前辈国王一样地位显赫，但却没有前辈国王的能力，不能为百姓造福。

第二，任何人都不能在一开始就拥有超越人们当时授予他的公共荣耀，献上这些荣耀的人也没有这些权力出让他们后代的权利。虽然他们可以（对他们认为贤明的人）说："我们选择你当我们的头领"，但是他们没有权利说："你的子子孙孙可以世世代代永远统治我们和我们的后代"。这无疑对这些对第一代君王献上荣耀的人们的后代是不公平的。因为这种不明智的，不公正的，违反自然的约定，可能使他们的后代处于一个粗鲁的，愚蠢的人的统治之下。大部分明智的人在内心的情感中，都鄙视世袭制度，但是一旦邪恶被确立就很难被清除，很多人屈从是出于恐惧，一些人出于迷信，还有一些人是掌权者阶层，他们可以与国王一起分享压迫其他人的权力。

假设现世国王们的家族都有一个光荣的开头，但是，当我们扯开遮掩在古代历史上黑暗的面纱，追踪他们起家的根源，我们极有可能发现他们的第一代只是一个无法无天的恶棍的首领。他们狡诈残暴、手段凶残之极，这才为其赢得了匪首的头衔。随着他们权力的扩大，老实的无助的人们不得不经常向这些头领奉献自己的一切，以求得平安。但是，君主的选民们并没有想到要给这些君主的后代们世袭的权力，因为这种永久的将后代的选择权排除在外的做法，是与人们赖以生存的自由和不受压制的原则相背离的。所以，在君主制早期，世袭制度并不是一种必然的规则，而只是在政权更替时的临时或辅助办法。但是，因为历史对于当时的情况很少有记录，而且传统的历史充满了没有根据的传说，在经过了几代人之后很容易流传古代圣贤的迷信神话故事，君主世袭权力就如此这般地强加给百姓了。人们也许担心当一个领导人逝去和选择新领导时产生混乱或可能产生混乱的局面（在流氓中进行选择是不可能不乱的），许多人开始赞成世袭制度。所以世袭制度就如此发生了并延续至今，在一开始时作为权宜之计的世袭方式后来变成了君王们自认为的一项权力。

　　英格兰自被征服以来，只有少数贤明的君主，大部分时期国家在数量更多的昏君的统治下呻吟。所以，没有任何具有正常思维的人不能够这样说，他们在征服者威廉[64]的统治下的经历是值得荣耀的。一个法国的混蛋带着一帮武装的团伙登陆，未经本地人同意将自己封为英格兰国王。这很明显，从开始这就是流氓行径，毫无疑问，没有任何神圣的意味。然而，不必花费太多时间揭露世袭制的荒

---

〔64〕　征服者威廉（William the Conqueror，约1028年~1087年9月9日），亦称为英格兰的威廉一世（William I of England）是英格兰的第一位诺曼人国王。他同时是诺曼底公爵。威廉于1027年或1028年生于法国诺曼底法莱斯的法莱斯城堡，是诺曼底公爵罗贝尔一世的儿子，同时是英格兰王后诺曼底的艾玛的侄孙，他的父亲仍指定他为诺曼底的继承人。他15岁时被封骑士，开始在领地执政。1066年向英格兰开战并于同年9月引兵渡海，击败了英格兰国王哈罗德的抵抗，同年12月25日，威廉在威斯敏斯特教堂加冕为英格兰国王，诺曼王朝开始。威廉一世即位后，将英国的五分之一土地作为自己的领地，将手下的骑士分别派驻各地镇守，并在全国修建了很多城堡。著名的伦敦塔和温莎城堡都是在那个时期修建的。威廉一世引入了法语和法国的生活习惯，其中一些词汇和习俗对英国产生了很大的影响。

谬，如果有任何人弱智到愿意认可世袭制，让他们胡乱崇拜和欢迎驴子和狮子[65]吧。我绝不学他们那样卑贱，也不想打搅他们那样愚忠。

　　然而我很愿意提出这样的问题，先民们起初如何设立国王的？这个问题只有三种答案，即要么采取抽签的方式、要么采取选举的方式或者采取抢夺的方式。如果第一个国王是由抽签产生的，而且这种方式成为国王产生的先例，那么就排除了世袭制。扫罗（Saul）为王是根据抽签而不是继承成为犹太人的王的，整个事件的过程中，没有世袭的意图。[66]如果任何国家的第一位国王由选举产生，并由此建立了抽签选王的先例。如果他们的选择不仅仅是一个国王，而是国王家族的永久统治，则可以说第一批选举者的行为剥夺了他们的后代的选举权利。这在《圣经》内外都找不到相应的根据，只是一种原罪条文可与之类

---

〔65〕　译者注：作者此处用驴子和狮子比喻人们所说的昏君和明君。

〔66〕　译者注：扫罗抽签为王的故事见《圣经·撒母耳记上》第 10 章第 17～24 节。《圣经》记载：撒母耳将百姓招聚到米斯巴耶和华那里，对他们说，耶和华以色列的神如此说，我领你们以色列人出埃及，救你们脱离埃及人的手，又救你们脱离欺压你们各国之人的手。你们今日却厌弃了救你们脱离一切灾难的神，说"求你立一个王治理我们"。现在你们应当按着支派，宗族都站在耶和华面前。于是，撒母耳使以色列众支派近前来掣签，就掣出便雅悯支派来。又使便雅悯支派按着宗族近前来，就掣出玛特利族，从其中又掣出基士的儿子扫罗。众人寻找他却寻不着，就问耶和华说，那人到这里来了没有。耶和华说，他藏在器具中了。众人就跑去从那里领出他来。他站在百姓中间，身体比众民高过一头。撒母耳对众民说，你们看耶和华所拣选的人，众民中有可比他的吗？众民就大声欢呼说，愿王万岁。

比，（世袭制剥夺了后代的选举权）如同所有人的自由意志都因为亚当而失去一样[67]。从这点可以看出，世袭制毫无可赞美之处可言。因为亚当，所有人都担负了原罪；因为第一批选民，所有的后人都必须服从；因为一个人的过错，全人类都屈从于魔鬼；因为第一次选举，所有的后代人们都必须臣服于世袭的统治；因为亚当，我们后代都失去了清白之身；因为第一批选民拥戴出国王，我们后代就永久地受制于国王的统治。以上两方面都使我们无法重新获得先前的地位和权利，它毫无争辩地表明：原罪和世袭制是同样的东西。两者同等卑劣！两者同等可耻！即使最精明的辩论家也无法给出更恰当的比喻了。

至于抢夺，即使最狡辩的人也无法为之辩解，征服者威廉是一个抢夺者是不容否认的事实。显而易见，英国君主制的历史是经不起查验的。

对人类而言，世袭制荒谬之危害远不如其邪恶。如果世袭制确实能够保证掌权者是一个善良和贤明的家族，神也许会同意他们掌握王权，但是，世袭制度却为愚蠢、邪恶和不合适的人掌权开启大门，其本性是对人民的强暴。世袭制使有些人自认为生来就应当统治他人，而他人生来

---

〔67〕　译者注：根据《圣经·创世纪》记载，亚当是人类的始祖，他和他的妻子夏娃因为违背上帝的意志，吃了伊甸园中的苹果而被上帝赶出伊甸园。亚当的子孙也因此担负起原罪，不能在乐园中自由地享乐，而必须终身劳作挣得衣食，并须经受生老病死的痛苦。

就应当被统治，这些人很快变得粗鲁傲慢。世袭制以选种模式选出的继承人，这种把一些人与人类其他人区别开来的模式使得被选的人思想早就受到毒化，他们自我以为很重要，自以为高人一等，他们处世的方式与世界上大多数人有重要的区别：他们很少有机会了解世人的真正利益，他们继承政府统治权力之后，通常对政府管理最无知和全方位不胜任。[68]

世袭制的另一个邪恶之处是，王位可能由任何年龄的未成年继承。在幼主当政期间，摄政者代行国王权力，他面临许多机会和引诱进行谋反篡权；类似的可能引起全民族遭殃的情况也发生在当国王年老体弱行将就木之时。在这两种情况下，谋反的恶棍可能成功地从将死的或年幼的国王手中抢得王冠，而人民大众只是他的猎物。

赞同世袭制最蛊惑人心的说辞是它可以使国家免于内战。如果这种说法是真实的，那世袭制也并非不可取。然而，这是有史以来施加于人类的最厚颜无耻的谎言。英格

---

[68] 1760年乔治三世在其祖父去世后继承王位。起初他雄心勃勃，想做一个贤明的君王。他废除了与之长期合作、关系稳定的辉格党的权力，组成了自己的政治同盟。但他新任的大臣具有先天不稳的特点，每人的任职期限平均只有两年。国王严重的智力和心理缺陷更加重了他政治活动的艰难。他经常出现间断性精神错乱，即使在1760年~1770年代还清醒理智的时候，乔治三世也显得力不从心。他一次次极力证明自己健康胜任，但一次次地发现多病躯体无法适应王位的挑战。所以，国王的个性对艰难岁月中不列颠政府的反复无常和极端顽固产生了重要影响。参见[美]艾伦·布林克利著，邵旭东译：《美国史》，海南出版社2009年版，第104页。

兰全部历史否定了这种说法的真实性。自从诺曼征服英格兰以来共有 30 个国王和 2 个幼主，在这期间（包括革命时期）共发生不少于 8 次内战，19 次反叛。所以，世袭制与其说制造了和平，不如说破坏了和平，并且摧毁了和平赖以存在的最根本的基础。

约克家族和兰卡斯特家族在王位和继承方面的冲突〔69〕，使英格兰成为多年来的血腥战场。在亨利（Henry）和爱德华（Edward）之间发生了 12 次激战和一些小的冲突和战斗。亨利两次成为爱德华的俘虏，爱德华也当过亨利的俘虏。这些出于个人因素而引发的征战，使战争的结果和民族的气数均处于动荡之中。亨利得胜时从监狱回到王宫，爱德华不得不从王宫逃往国外。但是气数的变换悠忽不定，当亨利从王位上被推翻，爱德华又被召回重登王位。〔70〕议

---

〔69〕　译者注：约克王朝和兰卡斯特王朝均是金雀花王朝的旁支，这两个家族的继承人争夺英国王位，导致了英国历史上玫瑰战争。战争命名的原因是两个王朝的家徽上均有一朵玫瑰：约克王朝的是一朵白玫瑰，兰卡斯特王朝的是一朵红玫瑰。

〔70〕　译者注：亨利（Henry Ⅵ，1421 年 12 月 6 日~1471 年 5 月 21 日）是兰卡斯特王朝的最后一位英格兰国王，在位时间为 1422 年~1461 年，1470 年~1471 年。由于他的软弱，英格兰在亨利五世时代取得的丰硕战果丧失殆尽，且陷入血腥的玫瑰战争之中。亨利六世是英格兰国王亨利五世和王后瓦卢瓦的凯瑟琳唯一的儿子，生于伯克郡温莎。当他的父王去世时，他出生后 9 个月，即被宣布为英格兰国王。爱德华（Edward Ⅳ，1442 年 4 月 28 日~1483 年 4 月 9 日），英格兰国王，1461 年 3 月 4 日到 1483 年 4 月 9 日在位。他是约克公爵理查之子。父亲理查在 1460 年战死后作为约克派首领。1461 年即位，1470 年亨利六世复位，他在法国军队帮助下击败了沃里克伯爵，并将亨利六世杀害于伦敦塔。

会永远服从强盛的一方。

这场冲突开始于亨利六世（Henry the Sixth）执政期间，到亨利七世（Henry the Seventh）执政时才完全结束，长达 67 年，即从 1422 年开始到 1489 年终结。[71]

总而言之，君主制和世袭继承问题使得整个世界（而不是个别王国）成为血与火的战场，这种形式的统治违背了上帝的意志，不可避免地给人类带来灾祸。

如果我们了解国王的所作所为，就会发现在一些国家里国王无所事事，懒散地度过一生，对他个人和国家毫无益处。当他们退下历史舞台，留给他们继任者的是同样的懒散生活。在君主集权统治机制下，国家的民事和军事事务皆系于国王一身。以色列的子孙在要求设立一个国王时，所要求的是："他可以统领我们，为我们争战。"[72]但是，在有些国家，如英格兰，国王既非士师，也非将军，

---

〔71〕　译者注：亨利七世（Henry Ⅶ，1457 年 1 月 28 日 ~ 1509 年 4 月 21 日），全名为：亨利·都铎，是英格兰国王，都铎王朝（Tudor Dynasty）的建立者。1485 年 8 月 22 日到 1509 年 4 月 21 日在位。为了缓和政治矛盾，并加强自己成为英王的合法性，1486 年 1 月 18 日，在伦敦的威斯敏斯特大教堂，亨利七世同约克王朝爱德华四世之女伊丽莎白举行了结婚典礼，他们原本就都是爱德华三世的后裔。亨利七世宣布约克和兰卡斯特两大家族合并，平息了对其继位的争论，更以这场敌对家族之间的联姻，结束了战争。

〔72〕　译者注：此句见《圣经·撒母耳记》第 8 章第 19 节。英文原文为"that he may judge us, and go out before us and fight out battles"。这里的"judge"一词有裁决纠纷的意思，在汉语中通常对译为"判决"或"法官"。《圣经》汉语本中将其译为"统领"反映了古代部落行政首领（统领）同时担任司法工作的职能。紧接着的下文中，作者说"英格兰国王既非法官，也非将军"，反映了作者所处的时代，英国的司法职能已经应当由"法官"行使。

人们不禁疑惑，他究竟是干什么的。

任何政体越向共和靠拢，国王的职能就越少。对于英国的政体，要给它寻找一个恰当的名号是很困难的。威廉·梅雷迪斯勋爵（Sir William Meredith）[73] 称它为共和，但在现在的状态下，它不配这个称号。英国王室可以随意安置各个官职，所以实际上王室有效地控制了全部权力，弱化了下院（政体中共和的部分）的功能。英国政体与法国或西班牙的君主制几乎一样，没有区别。人们为了国家名号争吵，却并不了解它们的真实意义。英国政体中具有荣耀的是其共和部分而不是君主部分，即人们可以自由地从他们中间选举下院代表。显而易见的是，如果这种优点不存在了，奴役则接踵而来。英国政体为什么出现毛病，就是因为君主制毒化了共和，王室侵吞了下院的权力。

在英国，国王所能做的只是发动战争和分封土地，一言以蔽之，他使国家陷入贫困和纷争之中。一个人每年坐享八十万英镑年金，并且还要受到膜拜，这真是一个好差事！然而，在上帝眼中，一个诚信的人对社会的价值比英国王室中的恶棍们更高。

---

〔73〕　威廉·梅雷迪斯勋爵（Sir William Meredith, 1725～1790）十八世纪时英国的政治家。

对目前美利坚形势的看法

在下文中，我只是提供一些简单的事实，清晰的观点和常识，并无过多的开场白，只希望读者抛开偏见和成见，使用自己的理性和感觉作出判断，并希望保有或者不抛弃作为一个人的纯真品格，扩大视野，不要只看眼前。

论述英国和美国纷争的文章已经连篇累牍。各个阶层的人们参与了这场论战，他们有着不同的动机和不同的目的。但是效果都不佳，现在论战阶段已经结束，国王已经决定使用武力作为最后的手段来解决这场争端，美利坚大陆已经接受挑战。

据报道，已故的贝尔汉姆（Pelham）先生 [74]（他是一位有能力的内阁大臣，虽然不是完人）在下院被攻击、被嘲笑说他的措施只是权宜之计之时，他回答说："这些措施在我这辈子够了。"如果这样一种致命的和不负责的想法主导了当前的美利坚之争，我们这代人的名字将为后代怨恨，遗臭万年。

---

[74] 亨利·贝尔汉姆（Henry Pelham, 1694 年 9 月 25 日~1754 年 3 月 6 日）第三位英国首相，在位 11 年（1743~1754）。也有翻译为亨利·佩勒姆的。这里借用亨利的话 "They will last my time."（"这些措施在我这辈子够了。"或者可译为"我有生之年当继续如此。"隐含着的意思是"我之后就不管啦"。）作者引用此句劝诫美洲人们不可安于现状，不可得过且过或不可固步自封。

太阳正在照耀着这一史无前例的伟大事业，它不是一个城市，一个郡县，一个省或者一个王国的事，而是一个占全世界可居住面积八分之一的大陆的事业。它不仅关系到一天、一年或者一个时代，这场争论牵扯到我们的后代，现在开始的这个事业将影响到永远。现在是大陆联邦忠诚、荣誉播种的时代。现在微小的分裂也将如用针刻在橡树皮上的名字，其疤疤将随着树的生长而扩大，后代读到的将是醒目的大字。

把争论的事项诉诸武力，开始了新的政治斗争的时代。一种新的思维方式生成了。在 4 月 19 日，[75] 即敌对状态开始之前的所有的计划和建议都如陈年黄历般成为过去，在当时可能适当的现在也已经过时和毫无用处了。当时争论的双方所主张的不管如何，都有一个共同点上，即与英国和解，他们之间唯一的不同是如何达成和解，一方提出使用武力，另一方主张利用友谊，但至今的状况是，第一种失败了，第二种的影响也退出历史舞台。

和解的好处已经说了很多，但和解如美好的梦想，已经离我们远去，我们却依然如故。所以我们应当重新审视对方的观点，并且深思与英国联合和从属英国，殖民地在现在和将来会遭受的许多重大的伤害。让我们根据自然的原理和常识来审视联合和从属的问题。以便清楚地看到，

---

〔75〕　1775 年 4 月 19 日美国独立战争第一枪在美国莱克星顿镇打响。

如果与英国分开我们将付出什么，如果从属英国我们将得到什么。

我曾听到有人宣称，美利坚过去的繁荣是因为它以前与英国的关系，所以对于美利坚将来的幸福而言这种关系应当保持下去，并且永远会有同样的效果。这种说法在逻辑上荒谬至极。我们也可以同样宣称一个小孩因为吃奶长大他将永远不需要吃肉，或者我们生命当中的前二十年所做之事后二十年也必须照做。这种似是而非的说法即使能够站住脚，我对此的回答是：如果没有哪个欧洲强权干涉美利坚，美利坚也可以一样繁荣，甚至更加繁荣。美利坚通过商贸而富强，商贸是人们生活所必须，只要吃饭仍然是欧洲人的习惯，商贸永远就有市场。

有人说，它（指英国）保护了我们。真实情况是它占有了我们，用我们的付出以及它的付出保护了这片大陆，然而，出于同样的贸易和掌控的原因，它也有同样的动机去保护土耳其。

啊，我们被古老的偏见引导得太久了，并且为迷信付出了太多的牺牲。我们一直夸耀大不列颠的保护，但就没想想它的动机是利益，而不是感情：它并没有为了我们而对抗我们的敌人，而是为了它自己的利益而对抗它的敌人，它所对抗的敌人与我们并无冲突，但因为我们与英国一体而成为我们的敌人。让不列颠别再对这片大陆进行保护吧，或者这片大陆抛开对它的依附。当法国和西班牙与不列颠开战时，我们可以与它们保持和平。上次汉诺威之战〔76〕所带来的灾难警示我们不要与英国牵连在一起。

最近有人在议会中宣称，各殖民地本无关系，只有通过母国才有了关系，即宾西法尼亚和新泽西，以及其它各地都是通过英国才成为姐妹关系的。用这种说法证明关联性太不直接了，相反用它证明敌对性则是最直接和最真实的。我们作为美利坚人，法国和西班牙从来不是，将来也不会是我们的敌人，但我们作为大不列颠臣民，它们才成为我们的敌人。

有人说，不列颠是祖国。那它的行为就更无耻了。即使野兽都不吞噬自己的孩子，野蛮人都不与他们的家人开战。如果英国是祖国这种说法是真实的，它将是对英国的谴责。但这种说法并不真实，或者只有部分真实。君主和他的走狗们总是狡猾地借用"父母之邦"或"祖国"一词，利用我们人性中轻信的弱点，以达到其卑鄙的、不公平的图谋。欧洲，而不是英格兰，才是我们的父母之邦。这

---

〔76〕 汉诺威之战即七年战争。它发生在 1756 年～1763 年。当时欧洲各主要强国均参与了这场战争，其影响覆盖了欧洲，北美，中美利坚，西非海岸，印度，以及菲律宾。这场战争由欧洲列强之间的对抗所驱动。七年战争最重要的战场不是在欧洲大陆，因此在那里只不过造成了微不足道的变化。它的主要战场在大西洋、北美以及印度。大英帝国与法兰西王国和西班牙帝国在贸易与殖民地上相互竞争。1763 年法兰西王国，西班牙帝国与大英帝国签订的《巴黎和约》（Treaty of Paris 1763），以及萨克森，奥地利帝国与普鲁士王国签订的《胡贝尔图斯堡和约》（Treaty of Hubertusburg）共同标志着战争的结束。这次战争总共造成了约 90 万至 140 万人死亡。

片新世界是那些在欧洲各地因为热爱公民权和宗教自由权而受到迫害的人们的避难所。他们逃难至此，脱离的并非母亲温暖的怀抱，而是魔鬼的迫害，特别是英格兰，正是它的暴政把第一批移民赶出家园[77]，至今还在迫害他们的后代。

在这片辽阔的土地上，让我们忘记360英里的（英格兰的幅员）狭小限制，在更广大的范围内建立我们的友谊，我们愿与欧洲的每个基督徒结为兄弟，并为这种博大的情怀而欢呼。

令人高兴的是，随着我们扩大与世界的交往，我们逐步克服了地方偏见。在英格兰各分立的教区中出生的一人，他的大部分交往自然地限于他同一教区中的人们（因为他们在许多情况下有共同的利益），他们以街坊邻居的身份加以辨别；如果人们在离家数英里之外相遇，他们就会抛开街坊的概念，转而成为同乡；如果他们旅行离开本郡，在任何其他郡相遇，他们就会忘记街坊和同乡的狭小区别，转而称对方为同一地区的人，但是，如果他们旅行到法国或欧洲其他地方，他们的地域认同就会扩大到"英国人"。同样的道理，任何欧洲人在美利坚或在世界其他地方相遇，都是欧洲人，因为英格兰、荷兰、德国或者瑞典，当与全欧洲相比时，在这较大的范围内，这些国家都成为一个地方，正如街区、城镇和郡县在较小的范围内的

---

〔77〕 此处作者应指从英国乘坐五月花号（May Flower）到美利坚的第一批英国移民。

划分一样，这些区分对于美利坚大陆的思想而言都显得太狭隘了。即使在本地〔78〕，也只有不足三分之一的居民是英国人的后裔。所以，我反对以"父母之邦"或"祖国"这样的字眼专用于英格兰，因为这是不真实的，自私的，狭隘的和不大气的。

　　承认我们都是英国人的子孙有什么好处吗？没有。现在不列颠已经是我们公开的敌人，这就排除了其他的任何称号。与之和好如初是我们的责任这种提法只是彻头彻尾的滑稽言论。现在王室族谱中英格兰的第一任国王（征服者威廉）是一个法国人，英国贵族中一半是法国人后裔，如果用同样的推理，那么英格兰应当属于法国统治。

　　关于不列颠与殖民地力量联合起来就可以征服世界，这种说法很多。但是，这只是假想而已。战争的结果难以预料，这种说法也毫无意义。这片大陆绝不能耗尽自身去

---

　　〔78〕　这里的"本地"（province）应指宾夕法尼亚州（Commonwealth of Pennsylvania），因为作者这本书是在该地的费城写成的。宾夕法尼亚州是美国东北部的一州，为立国13州之一。该州自从建立之初就以宗教自由和政治民主著称，在北美有很大影响。美国历史上的许多重要篇章都是在宾州谱写的。宾夕法尼亚州最早居住着几个印第安人部落，1643年瑞典移民在南部费城附近定居，称为"新瑞典"，1655年荷兰人战胜瑞典人控制了这片土地，1664年英国约克公爵战胜荷兰人，该地归属英国。1681年英王查理二世签署特许状，把这块地方送给舰队总司令小威廉·佩恩（William Penn），以偿还所欠他父亲威廉·佩恩爵士的16 000镑债款。并指定以"宾"的名字命名这一地区，同时应小威廉·佩恩的请求，加上"夕法尼亚"（林地）一词，形成州名，即"宾（佩恩）的林地"。宾州作为英国在美利坚的较早的殖民地，理应有不少英国人后裔，而作者以宾州为例说明英国人在美利坚大陆后裔比例不多。

支持不列颠在亚洲、非洲或欧洲的战争。

再说，我们为什么必须称雄世界？我们的计划是商贸，如果我们尽力做好这件事，就能够保障我们与整个欧洲的和平和友谊，因为整个欧洲的利益所在是美利坚成为自由港。它的贸易永远是它的保障，而它缺乏金银保证了它免遭掠夺。

我要质疑那些最狂热鼓吹与英国和解的人，请说明本大陆与大不列颠和解能得到任何一件好处，我重复我的质疑，一件好处都没有找到。我们的谷物可以在欧洲的任何市场出售而得货款，我们花钱也可以在我们愿意的任何地方进口货物。[79]

我们因为与英国的关系而遭受的伤害和弊端数不胜数，我们对于人类的责任，以及对我们自己负责，都表明我们要停止这种联系。因为任何从属或依附大不列颠都将使这片大陆卷入欧洲的战争和矛盾之中，使我们与那些本来愿意寻求我们的友谊的国家不和，并将使我们与一些我们没有利害关系的国家敌对。因为欧洲是我们贸易的市场，我们应当与欧洲的任何部分形成中立关系。美利坚的真正利益在于远离欧洲的纷争，但是当它依附英国时，就决不能置身事外，因为它被当作英国政治中的一枚砝码。

欧洲王国林立，难以长久和平。每当英格兰与任何外

---

〔79〕 此处作者用美利坚与欧洲的公平贸易说明美利坚在这些活动中并没有因为英国而得到任何好处和不必依附英国。

国开战，就殃及美利坚贸易，因为美利坚与英国有连带关系。下一场战争和结果可能与上一场不同，如果是这样，现在鼓吹与英国和解的人们到那时就会希望与英国分开，因为中立比参战更加安全。一切正当或自然的理由都要求我们与英国分开。被杀害者的鲜血和自然的哭泣都在呼喊："分开的时候到了！"上帝安排英国与美利坚相距遥远，这也是强有力的和自然的证据，证明一方对另一方的统治不符合上天的意图。对于赞成分开的观点，美利坚大陆被发现的时间也是有力的佐证，美利坚人口增加的方式更加重了份量。美利坚之发现先于宗教改革〔80〕，恰似上帝慷慨地为宗教改革后遭受迫害的人们预先提供了一个避难的场所，而他们的祖国已经不能为他们提供友好和安全的环境。

---

　　〔80〕　宗教改革（Reformation），开始于欧洲 16 世纪基督教自上而下的宗教改革运动。该运动奠定了新教基础，同时也瓦解了从罗马帝国颁布基督教为国家宗教以后由天主教会所主导的政教体系，为后来西方国家从基督教统治下的封建社会过渡到多元化的现代社会奠定了基础，因而西方史学界直接称之为"改革运动"（Reformation）。西欧的宗教改革都把矛头对准罗马教会对欧洲的大一统神权统治，要求通过改革建立适应于民族国家发展的"民族教会"或适应于资产阶级兴起需要的"廉价教会"。欧洲各改教运动历经许多流血战事，如 1610 年亨利四世被刺杀，法国再度内战，新教信徒大量逃亡。1618 年德国路德派因不满奥格斯堡和约被毁，由瑞典国王古斯塔夫二世（Gustavus II Adolphus）领导，与国内罗马天主教徒交战了三十年，1648 年签订威斯特伐利亚和约（Peace of Westphalia），双方重新和平相处。又如 1568 年荷兰北部的加尔文派信徒因反旧教与其统治者西班牙国王对战，到 1609 年终获独立建国与信仰自由。英国在宗教改革后的国教还带着不少旧教色彩，许多清教徒（Puritans）想再加以改革，使成更合乎《圣经》的信仰，却受到欲恢复旧教的国王查理一世逼迫残害，于是许多人逃至新大陆，即后来独立的美国。

大不列颠对这片大陆的统治迟早总会结束。一个认真思考的人会发现他所谓"当前政体"只是一个临时东西，瞻望前程，哀痛难免。为人父母，当我们得知这个政府气数已尽，难以支撑，以致我们给后代留下的任何遗产将都将不保，我们深感悲哀。显而易见的道理表明，当我们使下一代背上债务，我们就应当为此承担责任，否则我们就是可耻和可悲地利用了我们的后代。为了明确我们这一代人所承担的责任范围，我们应当为我们的孩子提供帮助，我们应当把我们人生中承担责任的时间再向后移动几年。从这个角度出发，我们才能看到前景，但是我们现在因为偏见和恐惧而看不到将来。

虽然我小心地避免对任何人不必要的冒犯，但我还是倾向于相信所有赞同和解的人可以归入如下几列：不可信赖的既得利益之人；没有眼光的弱小之人；不愿正视的偏见之人；还有一些把欧洲想得太好的一些中间人。最后这部分人因为错误判断，从而对这个大陆的灾难而言比其他三类人更大。

远离灾祸之地而居的人们是多么幸运啊〔81〕，他们不必如美洲人民那样担心厄运临门，担心所有的财产没有保障，而如今美利坚的所有财产都处于这种没有保障的状

〔81〕 原文为："It is the good fortune of many to live distant from the scene of sorrow"。这种句式实际上是否定句，即"远离灾祸而居对许多人而言是很不易得的幸运"，进而可以理解为"很少有人能够远离灾祸，置身事外"。

态。让我们想想波士顿吧，那里的灾难会让我们聪明起来，让我们永远抵制不可信任的强权。那座不幸城市的居民们几个月前还过着平安和富足的生活，而他们现在只能在家挨饿或出门乞讨。他们如果继续留在城里，有被同伴打死的危险性；他们如果离开城市，有被军队抢劫的危险。他们现在的状况有如毫无救赎希望的囚徒，如果为了救助他们而发动攻击，他们又会暴露在双方的火力之下。[82]

　　缺乏血性之人对于不列颠的暴行看得太轻松了，对未来仍然抱有希望。他们还能大声呼喊："来吧，来吧，尽管发生了这一切，我们还是朋友。"但是，让我们考察人类的情感，让和议受自然试金石检验，然后再告诉我，你是否还能热爱、尊敬在你的土地上杀人放火的政权，并且还忠心耿耿地为它服务？如果这些事情你都做不到，那么你只是在欺骗自己，而且因为你的拖延将会贻祸于你的后

---

　　〔82〕　波士顿（Boston）是美国马萨诸塞州的首府和最大城市，也是新英格兰地区的最大城市，位于美国东北部大西洋沿岸，创建于 1630 年，是美国最古老、最有文化价值的城市之一。1775 年 4 月 19 日，驻波士顿英军奉命去康科德查抄殖民地民兵的军火，往返途中在莱克星顿附近遭殖民地民兵伏击，莱克星顿之战揭开美国独立战争（1775～1778）战争序幕。1775 年 5 月，各殖民地民兵主动进攻，先后攻占泰孔德罗加堡、克朗波因特等地，并围困波士顿。1775 年 6 月 17 日，马萨诸塞总督、英军统帅 T. 盖奇派兵 2200 名，向围困波士顿的民兵阵地邦克山和布里德山多次发起进攻。民兵英勇抗击，两次击退英军进攻，虽因弹药耗尽放弃阵地。在双方拉锯战期间，战火之中的波士顿居民处境非常困难。

代。你既不能爱不列颠，对它的尊敬也只是被迫的和不自然的，只是现在的权宜之计而已，那么你还跟不列颠绑在一起就会很快沉沦到比以前更惨的境地。如果你说你能够忍受这些伤害，那么我问你：你的房子被烧毁过吗？你的财产曾在你的眼前被毁坏吗？你的妻儿没有睡觉的床铺或者没有果腹的面包吗？你的父母儿女是否曾经命丧他们之手？最后只留下你孤苦伶仃，苦度劫后余生？如果你没有经过这一切，那么你不能评判那些经历过这些苦难的人们；如果你经历过这一切，你仍然能够与那些刽子手们握手言欢，那么你不配称为丈夫、父亲、朋友、爱人，不管你的地位如何，职位如何，你只是一个懦夫和奴才而已。

这些话并非煽情或夸大其词，而只是根据自然的正当情感所作的判断。没有这些情感，我们就不能履行我们的社会责任，也不能享受人生的幸福。我无意宣扬恐怖并挑起仇恨，而只是想把人们从昏睡中唤醒，这样我们可以坚定地追求既定的目标。如果美利坚没有被自己的拖延和怯懦所征服，那么不列颠或欧洲强权就不能征服美利坚。今年冬天就是一个可以利用的时刻，如果失去或忽略时机，整个大陆都将陷入不幸。任何人，不管他是谁，从事何职业，身在何地，如果浪费如此宝贵和可用的时机，受到怎样的惩罚都不为过。

认为这片大陆还能够继续臣服于任何外部政权，是没有道理的，是违反天理人情的。即使不列颠最自信的人也不作此想。如果不与英国分离，竭尽人类智力此时也无力保得大陆一年平安。和解无论是在过去或现在只是一个荒诞的梦想。上天已经抛弃了与英国的关系，人力又岂能挽回。正如弥尔顿所言："当致命的仇恨之伤痕如此之深，不可能再出现真正的和解。"[83]

　　各种平静的获得和平的方式都是无效果的。我们的请愿被羞辱地拒绝，这只能使我们相信，一再的请愿都是徒劳的，只是一次次证明国王是铁石心肠，只能证明欧洲国王们的顽固，丹麦和瑞典就是证明。既然只有奋起反抗是唯一出路，看在上帝的份上，让我们最终与英国分离吧，不要让后代人在被强加的、无意义的父子的名义下被宰杀。

　　"他们再不会作恶了"，这种说法只是愚蠢的幻想。我们曾在废除印花税[84]时这么想过，但就如我们设想国家

　　〔83〕　此句见弥尔顿《失乐园》第四章。约翰·弥尔顿（John Milton，1608～1674）英国诗人、政论家，民主斗士，英国文学史上最伟大的六大诗人之一。弥尔顿是清教徒文学的代表，他的一生都在为资产阶级民主运动而奋斗，代表作《失乐园》与荷马的《荷马史诗》、阿利盖利·但丁的《神曲》并称为西方三大诗歌。

　　〔84〕　1765年英国议会通过了印花税法案。该税法规定美殖民者所使用的每一份印刷品都要买一张英国的印花，这意味着美国殖民者必须为每一张报纸、每一份文件，甚至是每一张卡片都要支付印花税。《印花税法案》在美利坚街头引起了骚乱，民众纷纷发表激烈的反对演讲，斥责这一专制行为。抵制运动成功了。1766年，英国议会撤销了印花税法案，但是英国人和生活在其美利坚殖民地的人们的冲突远没有结束。英国终止了印花税法案，但并没有停止对税

被挫败一次就永远不会再起新的争端，一两年后，我们就会发现是被骗了。

在政府管理事务的层面，不列颠无力公正地处理大陆事务：这些事务很快会变得繁重琐碎，不能够由一个远离我们并且忽视我们的政权随便处置。他们既然不能征服我们，他们也不能管理我们。为传送一个报告或一个申请要跑三四千英里，等一个答复要四五个月，得到答复后，如果需要解释还得等五六个月。这些管理方式在数年之后将成为荒唐的笑柄。以前这样做是合适的，但现在正是改变这种现象的合适时候。

一些小的岛屿没有能力保护自身，可以作为一些王国照顾的对象；但是，认为一片大陆可以长久地被一个岛国统治，就非常荒谬了。自然界没有卫星大于它所属的行星

（接上页）收的需求。在 1767 年，英国国会批准了一系列新的税法，这些税法叫《Townshend Acts》（《唐森德税法》），这些税法的名称来源于一位提出这些法律建议的英国政府官员，《唐森德税法》针对从殖民地进口玻璃、茶叶、铅、油漆和纸张等商品进行征税。美殖民者拒绝执行《唐森德税法》，并开始联合抵制英国的商品，他们还努力加快殖民地制造业的发展。到 1769 年底，他们已经把从英国进口的商品减少了一半，美利坚殖民地还就他们自己的问题开始相互沟通了。在 1768 年，马萨诸塞法院给其他殖民地的立法机构发出了一封信，这封信说《唐森德税法》侵犯了殖民者的天赋权利和宪法权利。当这封信的消息传到伦敦时，英国官员命令马萨诸塞殖民地执政官解散立法机构，随后，英国又派遣四千人的军队来到波士顿。紧张情势不断升高，最后在 1770 年 3 月 5 日爆发了波士顿屠杀（Boston Massacre），英国士兵对着愤怒的暴民开枪，打死了五个人。美利坚殖民地的革命者们利用这个事件来激起群众反抗。《唐森德法案》在 1770 年被撤销，但英国政府把《唐森德法案》中对茶叶的征税保留了下来，作为某种象征性的政治宣示，表示英国还是有权力对其殖民地征税。

的道理，英格兰和美利坚的相互关系违反了自然界的常理，显然它们从属于不同的体系，英格兰属于欧洲，美利坚属于它自己。我支持分治和独立并非出于骄傲、党派或者不满等动机的诱使。我很清楚地、肯定地和明智地感受到它是大陆利益所在，缺少这一步的任何措施都只是修补而已，不能带来长久的幸福。我们此时自己退缩就意味着将战斗的任务留给我们的孩子。其实只要我们多做一点，走远一点，就可以使这片大陆成为地球上的光荣。

　　因为不列颠没有表现出一点点妥协的倾向，我们可以肯定（与英国和解）[85]没有任何条件值得大陆接受，或者没有任何（与英国和解）途径配得上我们已经付出的牺牲和财富。

　　争取实现目标总是要付出适当的代价。将诺斯（North）[86]赶下台，或者除去整个令人生厌的党派并不值

---

　　[85]　括号中的（与英国和解）字样为译者所加，下同。

　　[86]　腓特烈·诺斯（Frederick North，1732 年 4 月 13 日～1792 年 8 月 5 日），人称诺斯勋爵（Lord North），诺斯自 1754 年至 1790 年间在英国下议院任职议员，于 1770 年至 1782 年出任大不列颠王国首相。在任内的前半期，他着手处理北美殖民地日益高涨的独立呼声，后期则专注于美国独立战争。新任托利党首相诺斯勋爵及其政府对美利坚日益不满大不列颠的情绪十分关注，为了安抚美利坚殖民者，他撤销了向美利坚殖民地所征收的绝大部分税项，但却独留茶税一项。茶税对大不列颠十分重要，乔治三世甚至曾言茶税是大不列颠"保持（向美国殖民地征税）权力的一种税"，可是在 1773 年，波士顿人为了反对茶税而登上停泊于波士顿港的运茶货船，并将茶叶倾倒入海，以作示威，史称"波士顿茶叶事件"。有关事件在大不列颠引起了很大的反向，舆论对北美殖民者也出现不满。诺斯勋爵在茶叶事件发生后引入多项措施以作报复，当

得我们已经付出的巨大代价。使用临时停止贸易方法对我们造成不便，用此方式废除那些我们所不满的法案，并且这些法案确实被废除的话，这个代价已经足够；但如果整个大陆都必须拿起武器，如果每个男子都必须成为战士，所达到之目的仅仅是为了与一个可鄙的内阁斗争，那么我们的付出就太不值得了。如果我们的付出仅是为了撤销法案，如果我们全部的斗争也只是为此目的，那么代价太昂贵了。作为公平的评估，如果仅为了一部法律，而不是一个国家，付出邦克山战役[87]那样的代价就太愚蠢了。我

（接上页）中包括关闭波士顿港、修改麻省宪法，使当地立法机关的上院由君主委任产生，而不再由下院互选产生。这些措施进一步激起殖民者的不满，他们甚而称这些措施为"不可容忍的法案"，即 1774 年的《不可容忍法令》（Intolerable Acts 1774）。《不可容忍法令》包括以下主要内容：①波士顿港湾被迫关闭，直到波士顿赔偿"波士顿倾茶事件"的损失；②取消马赛诸塞州的自治权；③指控罪犯，并交由英国法院处理；④增加英国驻军数量，即"驻营法案"；⑤大片土地交由加拿大魁北克省管辖。美国独立战争期间，由于英军战败，诺斯勋爵在 1782 年 3 月 27 日辞职。

〔87〕　邦克山战役（Battle of Bunker Hill），美国独立战争中最初的流血战斗。战斗发生在 1775 年 6 月。数千名移民包围了在马萨诸塞波士顿的英国军队。英国托玛斯·盖茨（Thomas Gage）中将计划加强防卫在波士顿南的多切斯特制高点。美利坚殖民地军队决定越过波士顿以北的查尔斯河，占领在查尔斯顿半岛的邦克山。6 月 16 日夜，爱国部队加强防围紧靠波士顿的布雷德山，后备部队占据邦克山。次日清晨，英军威廉·豪（William Howe）少将率 2500 名士兵开始渡过查尔斯河。美利坚殖民地军队在威廉·普雷斯科特（William Prescott）上校的指挥下，随后赶到布雷德山山顶的防围线相持。英军发动两次进攻，均被击退。英军遂发动第三次攻击，美利坚殖民地军队弹药用完且得不到增援部队对邦克山的支持，因而撤出查尔斯顿半岛。战役共造成 1000 多名英国士兵和约 400 名美利坚殖民地军队人员伤亡。

一直认为，这片大陆的独立是迟早必定发生的事件，从近来大陆各方面条件迅速走向成熟而言，这个事件的发生将为期不远。所以，当敌对状态战事已经爆发，以此用来解决一件争议，而此争议假以时日就可以解决，那就太不值得了，除非我们真正想得到的仅此而已。否则，就如同浪费钱财打一场官司控告一个租约即将到期的房客的不当举动一样不值得。在1775年4月19日〔88〕之前，没有任何人比我更热切希望和解，但自从那天发生的事件开始，我永远拒绝那个冷酷的、阴沉的英格兰法老〔89〕，鄙视这个恶棍，他冒充"人民之父"，但对人民被残杀无动于衷，任

---

　　〔88〕 指1775年4月19日发生在莱克星顿美利坚民兵与英军的战斗。这一仗，北美民兵共打死打伤英国士兵247人，在激战中有8位民兵战士献出了自己的生命。莱克星顿的枪声，揭开了北美独立战争的序幕。

　　〔89〕 指英国国王乔治三世（George Ⅲ，1738年6月4日～1820年1月29日），全名乔治·威廉·弗雷德里克（George William Frederick），1760年10月25日登基为大不列颠国王及爱尔兰国王，至1801年1月1日后因大不列颠及爱尔兰组成联合王国而成为联合王国国王。乔治三世漫长的统治，见证了其王国与大片欧洲大陆进行的一连串军事冲突。在他的统治初期，大不列颠在七年战争中击败法国，并使大不列颠压倒欧洲各国，成功支配着北美利坚及印度地区。随着大不列颠在美国独立战争的战败，在美利坚失去了大量殖民地，这些殖民地的独立最终促成美国立国。法老是古埃及国王的尊称，也是一个神秘的名字，它是埃及语的希伯来文音译，意为大房屋，在古王国时代（约前2686～前2181）仅指王宫，并不涉及国王本身。新王国第十八王朝图特摩斯三世起，开始用于国王自身，并逐渐演变成对国王的一种尊称。第二十二王朝（前945～前730）以后，成为国王的正式头衔。习惯上把古埃及的国王通称为法老。法老作为奴隶制专制君主，掌握全国的军政、司法、宗教大权，其意志就是法律，是古埃及的最高统治者。这里作者把英国国王称为"法老"，表示英国国王不是当代明君，而是如古代专制统治的大奴隶主一样可憎。

他的灵魂在人民的血泊中安然入睡。

如果认为这些往事现在都已经了结，（而不继续战斗，争取独立）[90]结果将会如何？我的回答是"大陆被毁了"，理由如下：

第一，统治的权力仍然掌握在国王手中，他将否定大陆所有的立法。因为他一贯顽固地敌视自由，贪婪地独揽大权，他肯定会对殖民地说出这样的话来："**除了我允许的之外，你们不能制定任何法律。**"没有任何美利坚人无知到不了解：根据所谓的现行政体，殖民地不能制定任何法律，除非得到国王的许可；（根据以往的经验），没有任何人愚蠢到不了解，英国国王绝不容忍此地制定任何法律，除非符合他的意图。让美利坚无法可依或者让我们必须服从英国为我们制定的法律，这两者同样都可能使我们处于被奴役的境地。当事态平息之后（如宣称的那样），英国王朝会用尽全力使大陆处于低下和卑贱的地位，这点难道还有任何怀疑吗？除非我们继续前进，否则我们必走回头路，将永远地争论下去，永远愚蠢地提出请愿。我们的力量已经超过国王设想的程度，难道他不想努力削弱我们吗？一个对我们的繁荣怀有嫉妒的政权是适合管理我们的政权吗？任何人对此回答"不"，就是一个赞同独立的人。因为独立的意义无非我们能够制定自己的法律，国王

作为大陆最大的敌人不能再对我们说：**"除了我喜欢的之外，你们不能制定任何法律。"**

有人可能说国王在英国有否决权，没有他的同意，那里的人民不能制定法律。一个 21 岁的年轻人[91]（此事经常发生）对几百万比他年长、比他聪明的人说我不允许你们这个或那个法案成为法律，按常理来说，这很滑稽。此处我并不想对此评论，虽然我不会停止揭露它的荒谬，我只想说英格兰是国王住地，美利坚不是，这大有区别。在这儿国王的否决权的危险性和致命性比在英格兰要大许多倍，因为在英国，国王很少不同意增强英格兰国防力量的法案；但在美利坚，他决不会同意这样的法案通过。

美利坚在不列颠的政治体系中只处于次要地位，英格兰考虑这片土地的利益只是为了它自己的目的。每当美利坚的利益不能对英国有好处，或者存在一点小干扰，英国从自身利益出发一定会压制我们的发展。想想已经发生的事情，就知道我们在这样一个老旧政府的统治之下会很快变成什么样子！仅靠改一个名字，敌人不能变成朋友。为了表明现在和解的危险性，我肯定：国王废除法案只是当下的权宜之计，其目的是为了重新确立他对各州的统治。他深谋远虑，想用权谋的手段达到他在短时间不能用武力实现的目标。所以，和解和毁灭是连带的。

---

〔91〕　英国国王乔治三世生于 1738 年 6 月 4 日，1760 年 10 月 25 日登基为大不列颠国王及爱尔兰国王，时年为 22 岁。

第二，我们所能得到的即使是最好的条件也只不过是权宜之计，或者是一种受监护的政权，随着殖民地今后的发展，这种状态无法延续。过渡时期事物表象和性质都是不确定的和得不到保障的。有财产的移民不会选择来到一个政府不稳定，终日处在动荡和骚乱边缘的国家，当前居民中的不少人也会利用这段时间处理他们的财产，离开这片土地。

所有主张中最有力的唯有独立，即成立大陆政府才能维护大陆和平并保护大陆免于内战的侵害。我担心现在与不列颠和解极有可能接踵而来的是各地的反叛，其后果将比不列颠所有的罪恶更致命。

已经有成千上万的人被不列颠的野蛮行为所毁，（还有成千上万的人可能遭受同样的命运）。他们的感受与没有遭受痛苦的人感受是不一样的。他们现在所有的只是自由，为了自由他们牺牲了原来享有的一切，现在已经没有什么东西再失去了，所以他们蔑视屈从。另外，各殖民地如同一个即将长成的年轻人，在情绪方面对不列颠政府没有什么感情。一个不能维持和平的政府就不能算一个政府，那我们对它付出就毫无意义。英国的力量只是一纸空文，如果和解一旦达成，骚乱随之而来之时，我们能指望它做什么！我听到有些人说他们害怕独立，担心独立会导致内战。我认为这些人说话没有经过思考。我们的第一反应通常并不正确，现在的情况是，破镜重圆勉强联系在一起肯定比独立更令人担忧。让我从一个受害者的角度设身处地想：如果我被赶出家园，如果我的财产被毁坏，如果我的环境遭劫难，作为一个男人，不甘忍受屈辱，我一定决不同意和解，也决不受和解的约束。

各殖民地已经展示了良好秩序和服从大陆政府管理的精神，这足以使任何理智的人感到轻松愉快。任何人都不必担心一个殖民地会试图凌驾于其他殖民地之上，否则就太幼稚可笑了。

没有差别就没有等级，完全平等就不会产生诱惑。欧洲的共和国都是和平的（我们可以说永远和平）。荷兰和瑞士没有对外战争也没有内战。君主制的政体才真正缺乏长治久安，王冠本身对国内的恶棍就是巨大诱惑。王权统治的骄横和傲慢常常膨胀，以至在一些情况下与外国发生冲突，而共和政府更多的是根据自然原则所的组成，他们可以通过谈判纠正错误。

如果针对独立确实还有担心的话，那就是还没有制定相关的计划。人们不知道出路，所以对于此项事业之开始，我提出下列建议，同时我要坦诚的说我的意见未必很好，权作抛砖引玉。如果能把各个人的想法收集起来就可以成为重要的参考材料，有智慧和有能力的人就可以利用这些材料改进成有用的东西。

各殖民地的集会应成为年会，只有一个会议主席。代表更加平等，他们的事务完全限于国内并服从于大陆会议。

让每一个殖民地划分为6个、8个或者10个比较方便的区域，每个区派出相当数量的代表参加大陆大会，这样每一个殖民地最少可以派出 30 名代表。大陆大会全部的代表数将达到至少 390 名。每一届大会可以下列方式召开和遴选会议主持人。当代表们会面时，从 13 个殖民地中采取抽签的方式选出一个殖民地，然后再由大会通过抽签的方式从这个殖民地的代表中选出一位做大会主席。在下一届大会上从其余的 12 个殖民地中选出一个殖民地，上一届大会选举出会议主席的那个州不在其列。如此进行直到全部 13 个州都轮流到。为了保证所通过的法律都是令人满意的公正的，至少得到大会代表中五分之三的多数代表同意。在这种平等组成的政府中还挑起不和的人，只能与魔鬼为伍。

但是，这项安排由谁发起，或者以什么方式进行，这些细节特别需要注意。最合适方式应当是由统治者和被统治之间，即国会和人民之间的机构发起。就此可以召开大陆会议，其方式和目的如下：

国会得有 26 名代表形成委员会，即每个殖民地两名代表。第一个州的会议派两名代表，每州民众中选五名代表，可以从州的首府或城镇中选择以代表该州，为方便计也可以从该州两至三个人口最多的地方推举。通过这些来自每个州各地的数量适当的、合格的代表们，一起参加议事。在这样组成的会议上，知识和力量这两大工作原则可以达到很好统一。国会、大会，或者会议的代表们具有处理国事的经验，是有能力和有作为的出谋划策人，他们的整体经过人民的授权，具有真正的合法权力。

　　这些代表们在商量大事的时候，首先应当制定一个大陆会议章程（《大陆宪章》），或称殖民地联合宪章（与英格兰大宪章[92]相呼应）确定国会和大会成员和选举方法。在他们开会之日，首先厘定各处的职权（永远记住，我们的力量在于大陆而不是各地）。宪章的内容应当包含：根据良心的指引，保障所有人的自由和财产，更重要的是保障宗教活动的自由，以及其他应当包含的事项。随后上述大会解散，根据宪章选出的机构作为临时的大陆的立法机构和行政机构。愿上帝保佑大陆平安幸福。

　　对于代表我们在任何机构中行使以上权力或为类似目的的人们，我谨送给你们睿智的德拉戈内蒂（Dragonetti）[93]评价政府时说的一段话。他说："政治家的科学在于确定幸福和自由的真谛，那些发现使个人幸福最大而政府支出最少的管理模式的人，才值得人们永远感激。"

―――――――

　　〔92〕"英格兰大宪章"，通常称为"自由大宪章"或"大宪章"（拉丁文 Magna Carter，英文 Great Charter）是于 1215 年英格兰的一些贵族与国王订立的条约，作为宪法性文件，用来限制英国国王的权力，规定王权接受法律的限制及尊重司法。

　　〔93〕　加奇多·德拉戈内蒂（Giacinto Dragonetti）。意大利法学家，先后担任过检察官、法官。1738 年出生于意大利阿奎拉地区，1818 年去世于意大利拿波里地区。1792 年，担任西西里王国法官，1798 年到拿波里，1799 年参加拿波里革命，革命失败后逃往法国，1803 年再次回到拿波里王国，此时为拿破仑当政时期，1806 年担任宪法法院院长，并为拿波里王国内阁成员。有著作 A Treatise on Virtues and Rewards（《论美德与回报》）。

但是有人会问，美利坚的国王在哪里？朋友，让我告诉你：他在天上统治，不像英国的国王那样给人类造成灾难。但是即使在世俗的尊严方面，我们也不能有所缺陷，让我们确定一个庄严的日子颁布这个宪章，让它以上帝之声和神圣的法律为依据。让我们托起皇冠，让世界知道我们所赞同的君主只是法律，在美利坚法律就是国王。因为在专制的政府，国王就是法律；在自由的国度，法律就是国王；仅此而已，岂有他哉。为了防止今后任何滥用权力的现象，在这个仪式结束之时，让我们破除皇冠，把它分散给人民，因为它就是人民的权利。

拥有我们自己的政府是我们天然的权利。当我们认真考虑复杂多变的人类事务，应当坚信：在我们掌握立法权时，我们应当以冷静讨论的方式制定我们的宪法，而不是将这利益攸关的事拖延到不确定的时间和场合，这才是最明智和安全的办法。如果我们现在不作为，一些如马萨内洛（Masaniello）[94]一样的人可能出现，他们将利用人们的不安，纠集绝望和不满的人们，将政府的权力篡夺为己有，如洪水一般将这块大陆的自由扫荡殆尽。如果美利坚的政府管理权力重新交到不列颠的手中，动荡的形势对一些胆大妄为的冒险家是一种命运赌博的诱惑（也会起来造

---

〔94〕 马萨内洛（Masaniello, 1622～1647）意大利渔夫，是1647年那不勒斯反叛的领导人物。他在那不勒斯公共市场上鼓动人们反抗西班牙的统治，在造反的当天自己当上国王。

反并夺取政权）。在这种情况下，不列颠将对解决动乱无能为力。因为在它听到消息之前，致命的事件可能已经发生，我们将如同在征服者迫害下的不列颠人一样承受痛苦。你们现在反对独立，你们不知道你们在干什么：你们把政府的位置空缺就是为专制的长久统治打开了一扇门。有成千上万的人认为把野蛮和黑暗的势力从这片大陆驱逐出去是一件光荣的事情，这个势力煽动印第安人〔95〕和黑人〔96〕毁灭我们，这种残忍行径具有双重罪恶，它野蛮对待我们，狡诈对待他们（印第安人和黑人）。

---

〔95〕　在欧洲人移民北美之前，美洲原住民为印第安人。它们有不同的部落，这些部落之间时常发生残杀，其野蛮与残酷远非旧大陆可以想象。美洲新移民到达后也有与印第安部落之友好交往的故事。如1620年11月初抵达今马萨诸塞荒芜之地的"五月花号"的人们就受到当地印第安人的接济而度过第一个严酷冬天。美国的感恩节，便来源于纪念"五月花号"新移民与感谢马萨索德印第安部落的搭救之恩。新移民对土地等资源的开拓，与印第安人产生了矛盾甚至战斗。例如，1622年的包哈坦战争中，印第安人摧毁了弗吉尼亚88个移民定居点中的80个，首府詹姆斯顿被夷平；1675年殖民者发起"大沼泽地战役"，以200余人伤亡的代价剿灭近千纳拉干人；而几乎同时，"菲力普王之战"中万余印第安人进攻新英格兰，荡平了90个移民定居点中50多个，号称北美历史上印第安人发动的最大战役。在战斗中印第安人的伤亡大致是殖民者伤亡的一倍以上。最终殖民者只能靠分化、收买印第安人才免于失败。在北美独立战争中，绝大多数印第安部落都站在英国一边镇压独立运动，缘由仅仅是酋长们迷恋英国殖民者赠与的商品。只有极少数部落与起义者并肩战斗。

〔96〕　黑人本来不是美洲的原住民。16～19世纪，欧洲殖民者从非洲（主要是西非）劫运大批黑人奴隶到美洲，其中半数以上运入今天的美国境内，主要在南部诸州的棉花、甘蔗种植场和矿山当苦工，他们深受白人种族主义者的残酷剥削和虐待，经常发生逃亡或反叛的事件。追根溯源黑人与殖民地主张独立的人（通常的白人移民）的矛盾是英国等欧洲国家在美洲的殖民行为所引发的。

　　我们的情感曾经受到多次的伤害，使我们深感厌恶。我们的理性禁止我们信任他们，让我们与这些人谈友谊，是一件疯狂和愚蠢的事情。随着每一天的流逝，我们和他们之间的血脉纽带日渐减弱，难道还有任何理由希望在我们的关系结束之际我们对他们的情感会有所增加，或者在我们在与他们发生前所未有的巨大矛盾之时，我们还能与他们更好地和睦相处？

　　那些劝我们（与英国）和睦和和解的人们，你们能够使我们回到过去的时光吗？你们能够给妓女以前的贞操吗？（如果不能）所以你们也不能使不列颠和美利坚和解。最后的纽带已经破裂，英格兰人正在反对我们，有些伤害是天理难容的，如果天理能容就没有天理。如果一个男人能够原谅强暴他的爱人的恶棍，这片大陆就能原谅不列颠的谋杀者。万能的上帝为了使我们善良和智慧，在我们心中植入不可磨灭的情感，这些情感守护着我们心中上帝的形象，使我们与野兽有所区别。如果我们对爱的情感触动无动于衷，社会契约就会解体，公正就会从世界上消失或者只能偶尔出现。如果我们心灵受到的伤害不能激起我们实现正义，那么强盗和凶手就会逍遥法外。

　　热爱人类的人们啊，你们敢于反抗暴政和暴君，请站出来吧！旧世界处处都充满了压迫，全世界都在猎杀自由。亚洲和非洲长久以来抵制自由，欧洲将自由视为异端，而英格兰对自由发出离开的警告。啊，接受追求自由的人吧，请及时地为人类准备一个避难的场所。[97]

---

〔97〕　此处作者号召殖民地独立成为一个新的国家，以接受追求自由的人们。他的这种思想后来在美国自由女神像基座镌刻的犹太女诗人爱玛·拉扎露丝的十四行诗《新巨人》中有所体现。"Keep ancient lands your storied pomp!" cries she with silent lips. "Give me your tired your poor, Your huddled masses yearning to breathe free, The wretched refuse of your teeming shore. Send these, the homeless, tempest – tossed to me. I lift my lamp beside the golden door!"（"让旧世界把你疲惫不堪的人、你的穷人，你挤在贫民窟中渴望呼吸自由的众生，你欲推到大海中拥挤在海滩上悲惨的人们，给我吧，送给我那些在风浪中颠簸的无家的人们。我在金色大门高举我的明灯!"）

论美利坚当前能力和我的一些思考

我所见到的人，无论是在英格兰或美利坚，都认为这两者之间的分裂是迟早一定会发生的。然而在我们努力探讨的关于大陆独立的条件成熟程度和适当性问题的方面，我们还缺乏结论。

既然所有的人都认可独立之事，只是在实施的时机上存在不同。为了消除错误，让我们对事情作一个大体的考察，如果可能的话，努力发现恰当的时机。但是，我们无需长篇大论，因为考察马上就会终止，因为时机已经找上了我们。发生的各种情况和各种事情完美的结合，证明了这个事实。

我们的伟大力量不在于数量而在于团结。目前我们在数量上也足以击退世界上任何武装力量。现在这片大陆已经有世界上最强大的武装力量和纪律严明的军队，目前我们的力量正处于这样的状态：任何一个单独的殖民地都没有能力自保，但如果联合起来，就能够完成此事，而且可能最为有效。我们地面武装力量已经足够，至于海上事务，我们不能忘记，只要大陆仍然掌控在大不列颠手上，它就绝不会容忍美利坚建立自己的海军。所以，（如果我们不独立），在海军方面即使一百年后我们也不能有所发展。

而且真实情况是，我们甚至更加削弱，因为大陆的木材每日都在减少，以至最终所余的木料都地处偏远并很难采集。

当大陆居民过多而拥挤时，我们在当前情况下的困难将变得不可忍受。如果我们有更多的海港城市，我们要保护的城市数量也就越多或者失去的数量也会越多。很欣慰的是，我们现在的数量正好与我们现在的需求相当，没有任何人是多余的。商贸的减少为建立一支军队提供了兵源，而军队的需求又创造了新的商贸。

我们现在没有债务，如果我们为此项事业而承担任何债务也将成为我们德行的光荣记录。只要我们能够给后代留下一个形态稳定的政府，以及该政府独立的构架，为此我们付出任何代价都不为过。但是，如果花费如此巨大只为了撤销一些邪恶的法案和废黜当下的政府，这些花费就太不值得了。这是对后代最残酷的利用，因为这是把最艰巨的工作留给他们去做，把债务加诸他们身上，而他们从中得不到任何益处。这种想法不是一个有荣誉的男人所应有，而是一个没有决断的心胸狭窄的政客的特征。

如果我们的任务能够完成，我们可能承担的债务不值得我们担心。没有任何国家不应当有债务。一个国家的债务是一种国家债券而已，如果不承担利息，则没有什么可担忧的。不列颠承担的债务高达一亿四千万英镑，为此，它付的利息就高达四百万镑。作为对它债务的补偿，它有一支庞大的海军。美利坚没有债务，也没有海军。只要有英国债务的二十分之一，就可以建立一支同样庞大的海军。目前英国海军的总价值最多值三百五十万英镑。

本书的第一版和第二版都没有包含以下计算，现在给出以下计算以证明以上关于海军的估算是正确的。参见恩蒂克（Entick）著《海军史》，引言，第56页。[98]

建造每个等级的舰船的费用，以及配备桅杆、船桁、船帆、缆绳，加上水手和木匠们八个月的海上供给，根据海军大臣布切特（Burchett）[99]先生的计算，费用如下：

建造一艘船舰按配备火炮数	花费英镑
100	35,553
90	29,886
80	23,638
70	17,785
60	14,197
50	10,606
40	7,558
30	5,846
20	3,710

从以上数据可以很容易地算出不列颠海军的总价或者

---

〔98〕 恩蒂克（John Entick，1703～1773）英国作家。《海军史》（*New Naval History*）于1757年在伦敦出版。

〔99〕 布切特（Josiah Burchett，1666～1746）曾任英国海军大臣近50年之久（1694年9月～1742年10月）。

成本，在 1757 年它最鼎盛时由下列船舰和火炮所组成：

船舰	装备火炮	单只成本（英镑）	成本合计（英镑）
6	100	35,553	213,318
12	90	29,886	358,632
12	80	23,638	283,656
43	70	17,785	764,755
35	60	14,197	496,895
40	50	10,606	424,240
45	40	7,558	340,110
58	20	3,710	215,180
另有与之配套的单桅纵帆船、弹药船，火攻船等共 85 艘		2,000	170,000
			以上合计 3,266,786
其他火器			233,214
			总计 3,500,000

　　世上任何国家都不如美利坚得天独厚，仅凭内部力量就可以打造一个舰队。柏油、木料、钢铁和绳索是它的自然出产。我们不需要去外国求得任何物品。荷兰依靠将它的战船租给西班牙和葡萄牙获取大量的利润，但荷兰造船需要进口造船所用的大部分材料。既然这片土地上的自然资源能够生产出一支舰队，我们就可以如同制造一件商品建造舰队。海军建成的价值大于其成本，我们还可以从中获得利润。将国家的商业行为和国防结合起来是一个非常

好的国策。让我们建立舰队吧，如果我们不需要我们还可以出售。这样我们就可以得到真金白银来抵消我们所花去的纸币。

在为舰队配备人员方面，人们通常有很大的误解。专业水手可以不超过船员的四分之一。那艘"恐怖号私掠船"[100]在上次战争中，在"死亡船长"[101]的指挥下经历了最激烈的战斗。在最后一场战斗中船上只有不足20名水手能坚守岗位，而该船编制人员达到200人。所以，只要有少数有能力和善于协作的水手就可以指导大量的非海上专业人员在船上完成日常工作。我们现在正是有能力开始

---

[100] "私掠船"（Privateer）又称武装民船，是一种获得国家授权可以拥有武装的民用船只，用来攻击和掠夺敌国的商船甚至军舰，其实质是国家支持的海盗行为。早在1243年，英国国王亨利三世就授予3条私人船只向法国人开战的资格。英国人一直认为，使用这种武装民船去困扰敌人是最有效、最便宜的办法。后来很多国家的政府都使用这些许可证作为国家工具来加强海军，可以使本国在不增加预算情况下，利用民间船只攻击敌国商船。在相当长时间里，私掠船是国家海军力量的一种补充。1856年，许多国家在巴黎签订声明，终止了私掠许可证的使用。美国和其他几个国家后来才签署该条约。因为他们缺少强大的海军，还需要依靠私掠来壮大他们的海上力量。恐怖号（The Terrible）是英国的一艘私掠船，装备有26火炮和200船员，在号称为"死亡船长"（Captain Death）的指挥下于1756年12月23日与一艘庞大的法国船亚历山大号（The Grand Alexander）交火，经过激烈战斗在只剩40名船员的情况下取得了胜利。在抢夺了战利品驶回英国的途中与法国的私掠船遭遇，经过激烈战斗，最终不支，恐怖号为对方击败，船长阵亡，船上存活者不足26人，其中16人肢体残缺，其他人也身受重伤，受重创的船的残骸漂浮在水中，已经无法被敌船拖走。

[101] "死亡船长"（Captain William Death），英国18世纪的私掠船长，死于1756年的海战。潘恩年轻时曾打算加入"死亡船长"率领的私掠船当一名水手，但被他父亲劝阻。

海上事业的时候，我们的木材是现成的，我们的渔业受到封锁，我们的水手和船上的工作人员正在失业。四十年前，我们在新英格兰就建立过具有七八十支火器的队伍，为什么现在不能？造船是美利坚最大的骄傲，在这方面它有望超越整个世界。东方的伟大帝国主要是内陆国家，从而排除了与美利坚竞争的可能。非洲还处于未开化状态，欧洲任何国家没有如此长的海岸线和如此丰富的内部物品供给。大自然提供某件有利条件时总是在另一方面有所欠缺，但它对美利坚如此慷慨地给予两项。幅员广大的俄罗斯帝国几乎与大海隔绝，它的无尽的森林、柏油、钢铁和缆绳只能用作商贸产品。

从安全的角度看，难道我们不该有一个舰队吗？我们现在已经不是六十年前那样的小国寡民了，那时候可以路不拾遗，夜不闭户。现在情况不一样了，随着我们财产增加，我们对财产的保护方式也必须相应增加。一年之前，一个普通的海盗沿特拉华河长驱直入，对费城任意劫掠，这种事情在其他地方也可能发生，胆大妄为之徒驾驶一只配有十四或十六件火器的双桅船就可以抢劫整个大陆，席卷数十万钱财。这种情况需要我们高度重视，显示了我们需要海防的必要性。

有些人可能会说，我们在与英国和好之后，它会保护我们。我们是否愚蠢到以为英国将海军驻扎在我们的海港中是为了保护我们？常识告诉我们，这个一直努力压制我们的强权绝不会保护我们。在友谊的伪装之下可能更容易征服，我们经过长期英勇的抵抗之后可能被欺骗而成为奴隶。如果不让英国的舰队进入我们的港口，请问，它如何保护我们？一支在三四千英里之外的舰队对我们而言没有什么用处，在紧急情况下，则毫无作用。所以，如果我们必须得到保护，我们为什么不自己保护自己？为什么要假手于人？

英国战船的名册很长，很令人可怕，但是，其中只有不足十分之一可以随时服役，许多已经不复存在，一些船只哪怕只剩下一块船板，它们的名字仍然在列。在可以服役的船只中，又只有不到五分之一的可以在指定时间停靠于某港口。东印度、西印度、地中海、非洲以及不列颠之利益延伸到的其他地方都需要它的海军保护。出于偏见和无知，我们对英国海军形成错误的认识，以为我们必须同时与它的全部力量抗衡，所以我们也应当有同样规模的力量，而这点在现在是不现实的。这种情况长期以来被一帮假托利党〔102〕人利用作为阻止我们兴建海军的借口。没有

---

〔102〕 托利党，英国政党。产生于 17 世纪末，19 世纪中叶演变为英国保守党。在 1679 年议会讨论詹姆斯公爵是否有权继承王位时，赞成的人被政敌称为"托利"。托利党人参加了 1688 年的"光荣革命"。1714 年汉诺威王朝建立后的半个世纪中，托利党在政治上一直处于在野地位。在美国独立过程中，一些亲英人士自称"亲英派"，人数不多，但不可忽视。把持独立的人士称他们为"托利党"。作者此处用"假托利党"人（Disguised Tories）讽刺美洲殖民地中一些不赞同团结一致与英国战斗的那些人。

什么事情比这种说法更荒唐了。如果亚美利加有英国海军力量的二十分之一，就可以完胜英国，因为我们没有也不需要谋求海外治权，我们的全部兵力将驻扎在我们自己的海岸。从长远观点看，我们有绝对优势，因为英国海军需要从三四千英里之外航行到此才能攻击我们，然后还要航行同样的距离休整和补给。虽然英国海军可以控制我们与欧洲的贸易，但我们也可以控制它与西印度群岛〔103〕的贸易，而西印度群岛是美洲的近邻，完全可以掌控。

　　如果我们认为没有必要维持一支常备的海军力量，也有办法在和平时期保持海军力量。如果给商人一笔费用让他们建造一些船只并配备20、30、40或50门火炮（酬金的数量与占用商人之船的吨位成比例），有五六十只这样的船，配上一些常备值班护卫，就可以形成足够的海军，而且不会对我们造成过大负担。英国海军负担过重，和平时期军舰在港口闲置的情形，广受诟病，我们不会发生这样的情况。把商业和国防结合起来是一个很好的策略〔104〕；

---

　　〔103〕　西印度群岛（West Indians）位于南美洲北面，为大西洋及其属海加勒比海与墨西哥湾之间有一大片岛屿，它是拉丁美洲的一部分。把这些岛群冠以"西印度"名称，实际上是来自哥伦布的错误观念。1492年当哥伦布最初来到这里时，误认为是到了东方印度附近的岛屿，并把这里的居民称作印第安人。后来人们才发现它位于西半球，因此便称它为西印度群岛。由于习惯上的原因，这一名称沿用至今。

　　〔104〕　此段作者建议给商人的费用（premiums，原意为保险费用）建造民用和军用的船只，以及称这是一个很好的策略（policy，愿意为保险合同），是以保险为例说明这项计划的操作原理。

当我们的力量和我们的财富能够相互作用，我们就无需害怕外部的敌人。

在国防的每一个事项方面我们都有充足资源，制造缆绳的麻到处都有，所以我们不缺乏缆绳。我们的钢铁比其他国家都好。我们的轻武器可匹敌任何国家的同类装备。我们可以根据我们的意愿铸造火炮，我们每天都在生产硝石和火药。我们的知识在不断进步。坚定是我们的天性，勇气从来没有消失。所以，我们还缺什么呢？我们为什么还犹豫不决呢？对于英国人，我们不能指望得到什么，期待的只是毁灭。如果英国一旦恢复了对亚美利加的统治，这片大陆就不再适宜居住。嫉妒总是产生，暴乱连续发生，有谁能够挺身而出平定一切？谁愿意不顾性命压制同胞屈从外国？宾夕法尼亚与康涅狄格州在一些土地归属问题上的分歧表明英国政府无关紧要，证明只有大陆的政权才能够管理大陆事务。

为什么现在是最好的时机的另一个理由是：我们的人口越少，未被他人占有的土地就越多，与其被国王浪费于赏赐他的无能的奴才，还不如我们利用于偿还债务和支持政府的日常开销。世上没有其他任何国家有此优越条件。

正如人们所说，殖民地正处于幼年，然而这并不是反对独立的理由，而是有利于独立的因素。我们的人口数量正好足够，如果再有所增加，我们就难以团结一致。应当注意的是，一个国家的人民越多，其军队的数量相对越少。在军队数量上，古代远远超过现代，道理很明显，贸易的产生是人口增长的结果，人们对贸易的热衷胜于其他任何事情。致力于商业活动削弱了人们爱国主义的情怀和武装反抗的精神。历史充分告诉我们，最勇敢的成就通常是由年轻的国家所取得的。随着商业的增长，英国失去了它的精神。伦敦市尽管有许多人口，却怯懦地一再屈从于持续的侮辱。人们可能失去的越多，越不愿意冒险。富人们通常是恐惧的奴隶，如同颤抖柔驯的狗一样屈从于王权的淫威。

个人和国家一样，其幼年时是养成良好习惯的时期。五十年后，这片大陆再成立政府，即便可能，也会很困难。各种不同利益，以及贸易和人口的持续增长，将产生混乱，殖民地与殖民地之间会发生冲突，各自坐大不再相互珍惜和支持。当傲慢无知的人为他们的一点特色沾沾自喜时，明智者不禁悲叹何不早日成立联邦。所以，当下是成立联邦的最好时机。年幼时结下的紧密亲情，共同苦难中结下的深厚友情，是最持久和难以改变的。我们现在的联盟正具有这两种性质：我们年轻，我们至今仍然遭受痛苦，我们同心协力共渡难关，我们在构建一个值得我们的后代引以为荣的时代。

现在是一个特殊的时代，对一个国家而言是仅只一次不可多得的良机，即自己组建政府的时代。许多国家错失良机，没有制定自己的法律，因而只能接受征服者的法律。它们先有国王，然后组成政府；本来应当先制定政府的制度或者宪章，然后由代表们执行。从其他国家的错误中，让我们接受教训，从而聪明起来——抓住当前的机会从开始就着手建立政府。

当威廉征服英格兰时，曾用武力强迫英国人接受法律。当我们同意亚美利亚的政府宝座被合法地占据之前，我们都处于危险之中，它可能被一些幸运的流氓占有，他们可能以同样的方式对待我们。到那时，我们的自由何在？我们的财产何在？

至于宗教，我坚定地认为保护所有真诚的宗教信仰者是一切政府不可推卸的责任，除了提供保护之外，我不知道政府还必须做些什么（即政府除了保障真诚的宗教信仰者之外不应当有任何干涉）。各行业的人都有一些心灵中的狭隘、自私的信条不愿意舍弃，如果一个人能够舍弃这些狭隘和自私，他就会立即无所畏惧。猜忌是卑鄙灵魂的伴生物，是所有良好社会的毒瘤。就我而言，我完全地、清楚地相信：人们之间宗教观点的多样性是上帝的意旨。这为我们的基督徒的慈爱提供了更加宽广的空间。如果我们都以一种思维方式思考，我们的宗教立场就缺乏检验的事物。根据这种自由原则，我认为我们中存在的各种不同主张就如同一个大家庭中的孩子们，不同之处只是他们的教名而已。

在第 37 页〔105〕，我提出了有关《大陆宪章》的性质的一些观点（我只是提出了一些思路而已，而不是具体方案）。在此，请允许我重提这个话题。我认为，这个宪章应当理解为加入的各个州之间神圣义务的契约，它支持各个组成部分的权利，包括保护宗教信仰、个人自由或财产。实在的争辩和合理的计算才能使友谊持久。

上文中我还提到了广泛的与平等的代表选举制度的必要性。这是我们政治生活中最应当注重的事情。选举人数量太少和代表数量太少对我们而言都是很危险的。但是，如果代表的数量不仅少，而且不公平，则是更危险的事情。作为例证，我提出了如下观点：当联合者〔106〕的申请送到宾夕法尼亚州议会，如果出席该议会只有 28 名代表，来自巴克斯郡的 8 名代表投反对票，来自切斯特郡的 7 名代表也投反对票，全州就被这两个郡控制了。这种由少数人决定的危险是经常发生的。类似的情况是，上次议会在未得批准的情况下取得了对该州代表的不正当的掌控。这些事情应当警示人们如何将自己手中的权力委托于人。那套对代表们的指导规则的理论和实践意义对小学生而言都浅薄得说不出口，可是这套规则在议会之外由少数人，甚

---

〔105〕 指英文本原著第三版第 37 页。

〔106〕 联合者（Associators）全称为"宾夕法尼亚联合者"（Philadelphia As-sociators），在美国建国之前是宾夕法尼亚保卫者志愿组织，在美国独立战争期间是宾夕法尼亚的革命组织，后改称宾夕法尼亚民兵（the Pennsylvania Militia）。

至极少数人批准了，并且带到议会中以"全体殖民地人民"的名义通过。如果全体殖民地人民知悉议会在制定一些必须的公共事务规则中塞入了那些不良的企图，人们会立即意识到这些人不值得托付权力。

紧急的需求使得许多事情成为权宜之计，但是如果延续下去则将会成为负担。权宜和正当是两种不同的事情。当处于危难之中的亚美利加需要议政，而当时没有现成的办法，或者适当方法只能是从一些议会中指定一些人进行这项工作，他们的智慧拯救了这片大陆免于毁灭。但是，我们不可能永远没有国会。每个希望良好秩序的人都必须懂得选择国会议员的方式值得慎重考虑。我请问研究人类的学者：让同一个机构拥有人民代表议事权同时掌管选举事宜，这种权力是不是太大了？当我们为后代计划时，我们应当记住：美德是不能遗传的。

我们经常从敌人那里得到一些极好的启示，而且我们经常对他们的错误感到震惊而变得理性。康沃尔（Cornwall）[107]先生（一位财政大臣）曾经蔑视纽约议会的请愿，他说，因为那个议会只有 26 人。他认为如此少量的人数不能代表整体。我们感谢他无意中透露的诚实。[108]

---

〔107〕 康沃尔（Charles Wolfran Cornwall，1735～1789）英国政治家，曾任英国下院议长。

〔108〕 如果有谁需要完全了解充足和平衡的代表数量对一个国家的重要意义可以阅读 Burgh's Political Disquisitions（Burgh James 的著作《政治研究》）。

总之，不管以下结论对某些人而言是多么奇怪，或者他们多么不愿意这么想，这都不重要，但是可以列出许多强有力的和显而易见的理由表明解决我们事务的最有效的是公开地和坚决地宣布独立，其中的一些理由如下：

第一，当两个国家处于战争状态，总有另外一些未参加争议的政治力量介入充当调停者并带来初步的和平，这是一种国际惯例。但是，如果亚美利加自称是英国的臣属，则没有任何政治力量，不论其对我们怀着多大的好感，能够提出调停。如此，我们将如现在一样永远争吵下去。

第二，如果我们只是想利用法国和西班牙愿意提供给我们的任何支持去修复裂痕并强化英国和亚美利加的联系，而去寻求这两个国家的帮助，这是不明智的。因为这些国家可能将受到不利的后果。

第三，只要我们还承认我们是英国的臣民，我们在外国人的眼睛里就只是叛乱者。臣民拿起武器这种先例对他们的和平也是危险的。既进行抵抗又要做臣民这种矛盾无法解决，除非有一个超出了人们常识所能理解的主意。

第四，如果发布公告，送达各国周知我们曾经遭受的苦难，说明我们曾经使用的各种和平方式进行补救都归于无效，同时宣布在英国朝廷的残酷统治之下我们不能幸福和安全地生活，我们不得已而有必要与英国断绝一切关系。同时我们还要表明我们与各国政府和平相处的立场，以及我们与他们建立贸易关系的愿望。对此大陆而言，这篇文告的效果要比向英国送出一船的请愿书效果更好。

目前我们在作为英国的臣民身份的状态下，无法被外国接纳，我们的意见也无法被听取。各国朝庭的惯例对我们不利，直到我们宣布独立与其他国家平等。

这些事项在起初进行时可能比较生疏和困难，但是，正如我们已经走过的其他步骤，在很短的时间内就会熟悉和容易。在宣布独立之前，这片大陆都如同一个人一样，将不容易做成的事情一天天拖延下去，但又知道此事必须要做，只是不愿意开始，然而又希望此事赶紧过去，从而一直纠结在此事必做的痛苦之中。

后　记

自从这篇小册子第一版出版以来，或者从它问世的那一天开始，国王的演讲[109]就出现在这个城市。仿佛冥冥之中有预言之神指引这篇成果的诞生，否则它的问世不可能是在这样一个最恰当时机和最需要的时候。一方的血腥意图表明了另一方追求信念的必要性。（国王的）报复使人们明白，（国王的）演讲没有吓倒人民，反而为果断独立的原则铺平了道路。

不管出于任何机动，对低级和邪恶的行为表现出哪怕一点点赞同迎合甚至沉默都是有害的。如果这个警句能够被接受，那么自然可这么说，国王的演讲作为一篇邪恶的东西应当得到，而且还会更加得到议会和人民的普遍憎恶。然而，因为一个国家的内部安宁很大程度上取决于可以称之为"国民素质"的高雅质朴，所以，通常人们以为最好使某些人和事物在人们的冷漠中自行消失，而不必动用人们不喜爱的新方法去抵制，因为新方法可能会对守望和平和安全带来未知的影响。也许正是出于这种谨慎的考

---

〔109〕　指英国国王乔治三世 1775 年 10 月 27 日对英国议会的讲话。其实国王的演讲早于潘恩《常识》的出版。因为当时英国离北美距离遥远，该讲话传到北美费城需要约三个月时间。

虑，国王的演讲才没有受到公开批判。这篇演讲，如果可以称之为演讲，是对真理、对公共福祉和人类生存的恶意中伤，是明目张胆地将人作为献给独裁者骄横的祭品。对人类的大屠杀是国王们的一项特权，也是存在国王们的必然后果。国王们不懂天理，天理也不容国王。虽然国王们的存在是因为我们的创造，但是他们不懂我们，反而成为高居创造者们之上的神。这个演讲也有一点好处，即它并没有企图欺骗我们，当然即使他想骗，我们也会不受其欺骗。它赤裸裸地表现出野蛮和暴政的面孔，使我们明白无误：该演讲的每一行每次读来都使我们坚信，在丛林中打猎、赤身裸体、尚未开化的印第安人都不如英国国王野蛮。

约翰·达尔林普尔爵士（Sir John Dalrymple）[110]，被认为是那篇阴暗的文章的作者，该文还虚伪地称为《英格兰人民致美利坚居民书》。他曾经自以为是地认为，如果这里的人们知道国王的真正品性（这对他而言是很不明智的）将会被国王的光辉形象和事迹所惊惧。"但是"，作者又说："如果你只有意对还说得过去的这届政府（指废除印花税的马科思－罗金汉侯爵[111]政府）表达敬意，而不

---

〔110〕 约翰·达尔林普尔爵士（Sir John Dalrymple，1726～1810），英国作家，曾担任过律师、法官。

〔111〕 马科思－罗金汉侯爵政府指第二代罗金汉侯爵查尔斯（Charles Watson－Wentworth，2nd Marquess of Rockingham，1730 年 5 月 13 日～1782 年 7 月 1 日），1765 年～1766 年任英国首相期间主持废除了印花税，但他同时认为英国有权对美洲殖民地征税。

对王国有所表示，是很不公平的。因为没有国王的批准，他们什么事情都做不了。"这是明显的托利党人论调，是明目张胆的偶像崇拜。任何人听了这种论调如果能平静地接受，就丧失了对理性的追求，自甘不齿于人类，这种人应当被认为不仅放弃了做人的尊严，畜牲不如，只配如同蛆虫一样在地上卑贱地爬行。

　　然而，现在不管英格兰国王说什么和做什么已经不重要了，他出于顽固的制度和残忍，已经恶毒地打破了所有的道德和做人的责任，践踏了天理和良知，引起公愤。现在美利坚的利益所在是自给自足，她已经有一个年轻的大家庭，她有责任管理好这个家庭，而不是抛洒自己的财产去供养另外一个有辱人类和上帝之名的政权。不管你们来自什么宗教派别，你们的办事机构应当守护国家的道德；如果你们想让你们的国家免遭欧洲腐败的污染，你们更应当守护大众的自由，盼望与英国分开。以下我将不谈道德问题，让其留给个人去思考，而就下列问题进一步阐述：

　　第一，与英国分开符合美利坚的利益；

　　第二，和解和独立，哪一个是更容易和最可行的计划？这方面我将略加评述。

　　关于第一点的论证，如果我认为合适，我能够提出一些在本大陆最能干和最有经验的人士的观点，他们在此问题上的想法至今尚未被公众所知。实际上，这是一个不证自明的情况：任何国家〔112〕如果依附外国，商贸受限制，立法权受束缚，都不能达到真正的富强。美利坚还没有达到富强状态，但她已经取得了历史上各个国家都无可比拟的成就。然而，与她将来可以取得的成就相比，现在的成就只是初级阶段而已，条件是如果她具有自己的立法权，这本来就是它应当有的权力。英格兰现在还在骄横贪婪地追求即使得到了对她也没有什么好处的东西，而如果本大陆还在忽略这个问题，听任其悬而未决，后果将是灭顶之灾。英格兰对美利坚的利益所在应当是商贸而不是征服。如果这两国能够如法国和西班牙一样彼此独立，这种重要关系将继续下去。因为在许多事项方面，双方都不能找到更好的市场。但是，现在独立于英国或者其他任何国家，才是最主要的、最值得考虑的事项，这一点，正如其他所发现的真理一样，日益清楚和强烈。

第一，因为独立迟早一定会发生；

第二，此事拖延的时间越长，成功的难度越大。

在公众场所和朋友私下聚会时，常常可以发现说话不经思考的人们的各种错误言论，我总是暗自好笑，不加点评。在我听到的诸多谬论中最常见的是，如果四五十年之后，而不是现在，本大陆与英国关系破裂，那么独立的把

---

〔112〕 此处"国家"一词英文对应的是"nation"。中文的"国家"一词在英语对应通常有三种，包括"nation"，指组成国家的人民，另有"country"，指一个国家所在的土地；还有"state"，指管理国家的机构。

握就大得多。对这种说法，我的回答是，我们现在的军事力量是从上次战争[113]的实际经验上获得的，再过四五十年就会消磨殆尽。到那时，这片大陆就找不出一个将军，甚至军官们也都已经不再有了，到那时我们，或者我们的继承人对战事完全不懂，如古代的印第安人一样无知。这种情况，如果仔细关注，将足以证明现在比任何时候都适合起义。对此，我的观点是：在上次战争结束后，我们获得了战争的经验，但是缺乏足够数量的武装人员；五十年之后，我们有足够的人员，但却没有战争经验。因此，最适宜的时间点应当是处于这两个时间中间的一个特别的时期，既有足够数量的经验的指战员们在世，而且新的战斗人员数量也增长了。这个合适的时间点就是现在。

　　请读者原谅以上跑题，因为在我开始思考这个问题时，上述问题还没有思考成熟，现在我再回到这个原来的问题上并提出以下观点：

　　如果修复与英国的关系，英国继续统治美利坚（在当前的形势下，这一点正在被完全放弃），我们就会失去偿还债务和继续借债的手段。由于加拿大疆界的无理扩张，有些省份偏远地区土地的价值已经被暗中剥夺，每一百英亩

---

〔113〕　指发生在1756年至1763年七年战争。当时欧洲上的主要强国均参与了这场战争，其影响覆盖了欧洲，北美，中美洲，西非海岸，印度以及菲律宾。七年战争最重要的战场不是在欧洲大陆，主要战场在大西洋、北美以及印度。期间大英帝国、荷兰、西班牙、法国等为争夺殖民地进行了多次战役，北美的居民也被卷入战争，从而形成了当地的军事力量。

土地的价格只有五英镑了，总价只值两千五百万宾西法尼亚货币，每英亩的土地税为一便士英国货币，每年为两百万。

卖出这些土地，我们可以偿还债务而且不增加任何人负担，保留的地税将变少，最终将全部用来维持政府的开支。只要土地可以出售，就不必担心何时才能清偿债务。国会可以临时担任受托人处理此项事务。

我现在谈第二个话题，即和解或独立，哪一个是更容易和最现实的计划，对此我简述如下：

顺应天理的人的观点是不容易被驳倒的。基于这一点，我的回答大致是：独立是一个至为简单的出路，掌握在我们自己手中；而和解是特别复杂的事项，涉及一个阴险狡诈的朝廷，结果可想而知。

美利坚当前的形势对每个有思考能力的人而言都是令人担忧的。没有法律，没有政府，除了建立在礼让基础上并因礼让而批准的机构之外没有其他任何权力模式。这只是出于情感因素而产生结合体，处于随时变化的不稳定状态，而且每个暗藏的敌人都在努力使其瓦解。我们现在的状况是，有立法机构而没有法律，有智慧而没有计划，有政体而没有名分，最令人不解和吃惊的是有完美的独立条件而却依附于人。这种情况史无前例，谁能预料可能发生的事情？在当前这种松散的制度之下，任何人的财产都不安全。多数人的思想不定，看不见确定的前途。他们追随煽动性舆论宣传。任何事都不是犯罪，人们不知叛国为何物，所以任何人都有自由为所欲为。如果托利党人知道生命会因为存在国法而被剥夺，他们就不敢聚众挑衅。应当区分在战斗中被俘的英国士兵和武装的美利坚居民，前者只是俘虏，而后者是叛国者，前者失去自由，后者应当处死。

　　尽管我们具有智慧，但在我们处理事情的进程中有些明显的弱点助长了分歧。大陆各部联结的关系太松散了。如果有些事情（指独立）没有及时完成，我们也失去了做其他事情的机遇，将陷入无论是和解和独立都不可能的状态。国王和他的那帮卑劣的随从们还在玩他们离间大陆的旧把戏，而我们之中不乏一些印刷商忙于散布这些虚伪的东西。几个月前在纽约的报纸上出现的那封伪造的、虚伪的信件（指上文所提到的《英格兰人民致北美居民书》），后来又出现在其他两家报纸上，足以证明有些人既无判断力也无诚信。

　　躲进角落里谈论和解是很容易的事情。但是，这些人是否认真想过这个任务多么困难，如果大陆就此分裂，又是多么危险？他们的意见中是否包括他们自己在内的各种人的各种情况的充分考虑？他们是否能设身处地为丧失了一切的受害人作想，为牺牲一切献身于保卫这片土地的士兵们作想？如果他们这种错误的温和决定只适合他们个人的情况，而不顾他人利益，那么事实将使他们相信：他们无权代表其他人作此决定。

有些人说，让我们回到1763年时的状态〔114〕吧。对这种论调我的回答是，英国现在也不能同意我们的要求，而且它也不会提出这种建议。但是，如果英国能够同意，并且批准了我们的要求，我想问一个合理的疑问：这个腐败的、不守信义的朝廷拿什么信守它的承诺？另一届议会，不可能信守，即使现在的议会都可以在事后废除它的责任，借口说这种责任是被强迫的，或者批准时是不明智的。到那时，我们的补救在哪里？诉诸国家法律将告状无门，大炮将是国王的辩护者；决定我们诉讼的将是战争的利剑而不是公义。如果回到1763年，只有法律回到当时的状况是不够的，还有我们的生存环境也要回到同一状态，我们被烧毁的城镇应当修复或重建，我们个人的损失应当得到弥补，我们的公债（用于防卫）应当免除，否则我们

〔114〕 回到1763年意味着回到北美与英国就印花税等事项发生冲突之前的状态。1763年法兰西王国、西班牙帝国与大英帝国签订的《巴黎和约》（Treaty of Paris 1763），以及萨克森，奥地利帝国与普鲁士王国签订的《胡贝尔图斯堡和约》（Treaty of Hubertusburg）共同标志着七年战争的结束。英国在战争获得了胜利，扩大了北美殖民地，但也背上了财政债务，需要通过向北美殖民地纳税来支付军费。七年战争后，英国政府为了进一步控制殖民地和镇压印第安人，派遣一万名军队常驻北美，由当地负责全部开支。1765年3月22日，英国议会通过了《印花税法》。经议会批准后的《印花税法》规定："殖民地的报纸、年历、小册子、证书、商业单据、债券、广告、租约、法律文件以至结婚证书等，都必须贴上票面为半便士至20先令的印花税票（须用硬币购买），违者将被送到不设陪审团的海事法庭受审。"对于这项《印花税法》，殖民地居民怨声载道，他们认为各殖民地的权利，是直接来自英王的特许而不是来自英国的议会，英国的国会里没有一个殖民地的议员代表，因此根本没有通过对殖民地加征税收的法案的权力，"无代表不纳税"成为当地居民反对课税的基本理由。

的损失将比我们处于那种所羡慕的时代坏上数百万倍。如果我们的要求一年之前就被满足，或许可能得到本大陆的衷心拥护，然而现在已经为时过晚，现在"卢比孔河已经度过"，再无倒退之路。[115]

　　另外，仅仅为要求废除一项有关财税方面的法律就拿起武器也不值得，就如同用武力强迫人们遵守这个法律一样，不符合天理人情。双方都不会为此目的而大动干戈，因为人的生命很宝贵，不应当为此小事而牺牲。促使我们拿起武器进行反抗的是威胁我们人身安全的暴力，是以武装力量摧毁我们财产的暴行，是对我们家园的野蛮侵犯。从这种反抗的模式成为必要的行为开始，我们大家不再是英国的臣民，从射向英国的第一颗子弹开始，标志了谋划美利坚独立的时代来临。事情发展的路线前后一致，不是随意画出，也不因为野心而延伸，而是由一连串的事件所

────────────

〔115〕"The Rubicon is passed."相当于"破釜沉舟，没有退路"。卢比孔河（意大利语：Lubikone）是意大利北部的一条约29公里长的河流。这条河源自亚平宁山脉，流经艾米利亚－罗马涅大区南部，最终在里米尼以北大约18公里处流入亚德里亚海。在西方，"渡过卢比孔河"（Crossing The Rubicon）是一句很流行的成语，出自公元前49年，凯撒破除将领不得带兵渡过卢比孔河的禁忌，带兵进军罗马与格奈乌斯·庞培展开内战，并最终获胜的典故。根据罗马当时法律，任何将领都不得带领军队越过作为意大利本土与山内高卢分界线的卢比孔河，否则就会被视为叛变。这条法律确保了罗马共和国不会遭到来自内部的攻击。因此，当凯撒带领着自己从高卢带来的军团（凯撒当时任高卢行省总督）在公元前49年1月渡过卢比孔河的时候，他无疑挑起了与罗马的当权者（主要是庞培和元老院中的贵族共和派）的内战，同时也将自己置于了叛国者的危险境地。直至今日，人们还用"渡过卢比孔河"或者"卢比孔河"这个词形容人们采取断然手段，破釜沉舟，并将自己投身于没有退路的危险境地的行为。

催生，画此线的作者并非殖民地人民（事态发展并非由殖民地挑起的）。

在结束这段论述时，我有以下及时的忠告：有三种独立方式需要我们思考，其中之一迟早一定会发生并决定北美的命运，它们是：人民通过议会合法的发声，诉诸武装力量或者由暴民造反。士兵并非永远是守法公民，大众并非永远是理性的人们，美德并非遗传也非永恒。如果独立是以第一种方式达成，我们有很多的机会和动力构建世界上最高贵的宪法。我们有重新开辟一个新世界的能力。自从诺亚方舟[116]到如今，从来没有如现在这样的情景。一个新世界的诞生近在我们手边，一群可能与欧洲人数相当的人们将从数月来的事件中享受到自由。每当想起这点都令人肃然起敬，与此世界伟大事业相比，那些少数的软

---

〔116〕 据《圣经·创世纪》第 6 章到第 9 章记载，创造世界万物的上帝耶和华见到地上充满败坏、强暴和不法的邪恶行为，于是计划用洪水消灭恶人。同时他也发现，人类之中有一位叫作诺亚的好人。耶和华神指示诺亚建造一艘方舟，并带着他的妻子、儿子与媳妇。同时神也指示诺亚将牲畜与鸟类等动物带上方舟，且必须包括雌性与雄性。当方舟建造完成时，大洪水也开始了，这时诺亚与他的家人，以及动物们皆已进入了方舟。《创世纪》如此形容洪水刚开始的景况："当诺亚六百岁，二月十七日那一天，大渊的泉源都裂开了，天上的窗户也敞开了。四十昼夜降大雨在地上"。洪水淹没了最高的山，在陆地上的生物全部死亡，只有诺亚一家人与方舟中的生命得以存活。在 220 天之后，方舟在阿勒山附近停下，且洪水也开始消退。又经过了 40 天之后，阿勒山的山顶才露出。这时诺亚放出了一只乌鸦，但它并没有找到可以栖息的陆地。7 天之后诺亚又再次放出鸽子，这次它立刻就带回了橄榄树的枝条，诺亚这时知道洪水已经散去。又等了 7 天之后，诺亚最后一次放出鸽子，这次它便不再回方舟了。诺亚一家人与各种动物便走出方舟。

弱、自私的人们的无端指责是多么微不足道和荒唐。

　　如果我们错过了当前的天赐良机，从而使独立由其他任何方式实现，我们将自食其果，或者责备那些心胸狭窄和偏见的人，他们不加研究或思考就习惯性反对独立。人们只要自己在内心认真思考，而不需要别人告诉，就可以得出这些拥护独立的理由。我们现在不应该再争论是否应当独立，而应当在坚实的、可靠的和光荣的基础上加快实现独立，并对独立尚未开始而感到不安。每一天都使我们坚信独立的必要。即使托利党人（如果我们之中还有这种人）应该是所有人中最热切期望推动独立的，因为开始指定一个委员会就可以使他们免于大众愤怒的伤害，所以一个明智的良好组成的政府将是唯一可以继续保护他们安全的方式。因此，如果他们没有辉格党人的美德，他们就应当有足够的谨慎并盼望独立。

　　总之，独立是能够将我们联合起来的唯一纽带。我们应当看到我们的目标，我们不能再听信狡猾残忍的敌人的诡计，我们应当采取适当的立场对待英国。有理由相信，就英国朝廷而言，自尊伤害较轻的方式是与美利坚各邦定立和约，而不是与它治下的反叛的臣民和解。我们的迟疑不决助长了英国征服我们的希望，我们的退缩只能延迟战争。我们曾经中断贸易以缓解我们的不满，但没有取得好的效果。让我们换一种方式，以独立方式自我治疗我们的创伤，然后我们可以提出开放贸易。英格兰的商界和有识之士将一如既往站在我们一边，因为和平进行商贸要比战争和没有商贸要好得多。如果这个提议不能够被采纳，我们可以与其他国家的政府进行交易。

至此，我就讲完了我的观点。鉴于至今未见有人对这本小书的前几版中所包含的论点提出异议，这从反面证明，这些论点无可辩驳，或者因为拥护者众，从而不能反驳。因此，与其我们以怀疑的眼光彼此注视，不如让我们向邻居们伸出真诚的友谊之手，结成统一战线。这条战线恰如一纸赦令，让我们忘却旧怨，让辉格党和托利党之分别不再存在，让我们不再听到其他的称谓，只听到"好公民、开朗和坚定的朋友、人权、自由和独立的美利坚的高尚拥护者"等称呼吧。

Common Sense

Thomas Paine

Introduction to the Third Edition

Perhaps the sentiments contained in the following pages, are not yet sufficiently fashionable to procure them general favor; a long habit of not thinking a thing wrong, gives it a superficial appearance of being right, and raises at first a formidable outcry in defence of custom. But the tumult soon subsides. Time makes more converts than reason.

As a long and violent abuse of power, is generally the Means of calling the right of it in question (and in Matters too which might never have been thought of, had not the Sufferers been aggravated into the inquiry) and as the King of England hath undertaken in his own Right, to support the Parliament in what he calls Theirs, and as the good people of this country are grievously oppressed by the combination, they have an undoubted privilege to inquire into the pretensions of both, and equally to reject the usurpation of either.

In the following sheets, the author hath studiously avoided every thing which is personal among ourselves. Compliments as well as censure to individuals make no part thereof. The wise, and the worthy, need not the triumph of a pamphlet; and those whose sentiments are injudicious, or unfriendly, will cease of themselves unless too much pains are bestowed upon their conversion.

The cause of America is in a great measure the cause of all mankind. Many circumstances hath, and will arise, which are not local, but universal, and through which the principles of all Lovers of Mankind are affected, and in the Event of which, their Affections are interested. The laying a Country desolate with Fire and Sword, declaring War against the natural rights of all Mankind, and extirpating the Defenders thereof from the Face of the Earth, is the Concern of every Man to whom Nature hath given the Power of feeling; of which Class, regardless of Party Censure, is the AUTHOR.

P. S. The Publication of this new Edition hath been delayed, with a View of taking notice (had it been necessary) of any Attempt to refute the Doctrine of Independence: As no Answer hath yet appeared, it is now presumed that none will, the Time needful for getting such a Performance ready for the Public being considerably past. Who the Author of this Production is, is wholly unnecessary to the Public, as the Object for Attention is the DOCTRINE itself, not the Man. Yet it may not be unnecessary to say, That he is unconnected with any Party, and under no sort of Influence public or private, but the influence of reason and principle.

Philadelphia, February 14, 1776

Of the origin and design of government in general, with concise remarks on the English Constitution

Some writers have so confounded society with government, as to leave little or no distinction between them; whereas they are not only different, but have different origins. Society is produced by our wants, and government by our wickedness; the former promotes our happiness positively by uniting our affections, the latter negatively by restraining our vices. The one encourages intercourse, the other creates distinctions. The first is a patron, the last a punisher.

Society in every state is a blessing, but government even in its best state is but a necessary evil; in its worst state an intolerable one; for when we suffer, or are exposed to the same miseries by a government, which we might expect in a country without government, our calamity is heightened by reflecting that we furnish the means by which we suffer. Government, like dress, is the badge of lost innocence; the palaces of kings are built on the ruins of the bowers of paradise. For were the impulses of conscience clear, uniform, and irresistibly obeyed, man would need no other lawgiver; but that not being the case, he finds it necessary to surrender up a part of his property to furnish means for the protection of the rest; and this he is induced to do by the same prudence which in every other case advises him out of two evils to choose the least. Wherefore, security being the true design and end of government, it unanswerably follows, that whatever form thereof appears most likely to ensure it to us, with the least expence and greatest benefit, is preferable to all others.

In order to gain a clear and just idea of the design and end of government, let us suppose a small number of persons settled in some sequestered part of the earth, unconnected with the rest, they will then represent the first peopling of any country, or of the world. In this state of natural liberty, society will be their first thought. A thousand motives will excite them thereto, the strength of one man is so unequal to his wants, and his mind so unfitted for perpetual solitude, that he is soon obliged to seek assistance and relief of another, who in his turn requires the same. Four or five united would be able to raise a tolerable dwelling in the midst of a wilderness, but one man might labour out the common period of life without accomplishing any thing; when he had felled his timber he could not remove it, nor erect it after it was removed; hunger in the mean time would urge him from his work, and every different want call him a different way. Disease, nay even misfortune would be death, for though neither might be mortal, yet either would disable him from living, and reduce him to a state in which he might rather be said to perish than to die.

Thus necessity, like a gravitating power, would soon form our newly arrived emigrants into society, the reciprocal blessing of which, would supersede, and render the obligations of law and government unnecessary while they remained perfectly just to each other; but as nothing but heaven is impregnable to vice, it will unavoidably happen, that in proportion as they surmount the first difficulties of emigration, which bound them together in a common cause, they will begin to relax in their duty and attachment to each other; and this remissness will point out the necessity of establishing some form of government to supply the defect of moral virtue.

Some convenient tree will afford them a State – House, under the branches of which, the whole colony may assemble to deliberate on public matters. It is more than probable that their first laws will have the title only of REGULATIONS, and be enforced by no other penalty than public disesteem. In this first parliament every man, by natural right, will have a seat.

But as the colony increases, the public concerns will increase likewise, and the distance at which the members may be separated, will render it too inconvenient for all of them to meet on every occasion as at first, when their number was small, their habitations near, and the public concerns few and trifling. This will point out the convenience of their consenting to leave the leg-islative part to be managed by a select number chosen from the whole body, who are supposed to have the same concerns at stake which those have who appointed them, and who will act in the same manner as the whole body would act were they present. If the colony continues increasing, it will become necessary to augment the number of the representatives, and that the interest of every part of the colony may be attended to, it will be found best to di-vide the whole into convenient parts, each part sending its proper number; and that the elected might never form to themselves an interest separate from the electors, prudence will point out the propriety of having elections often; because as the elected might by that means return and mix again with the general body of the e-lectors in a few months, their fidelity to the public will be secured by the prudent reflexion of not making a rod for themselves. And as this frequent interchange will establish a common interest with every part of the community, they will mutually and naturally sup-port each other, and on this (not on the unmeaning name of king) depends the strength of government, and the happiness of the governed.

Here then is the origin and rise of government; namely, a mode rendered necessary by the inability of moral virtue to govern the world; here too is the design and end of government, viz. freedom and security. And however our eyes may be dazzled with show, or our ears deceived by sound; however prejudice may warp our wills, or interest darken our understanding, the simple voice of nature and of reason will say, it is right.

I draw my idea of the form of government from a principle in nature, which no art can overturn, viz. that the more simple any thing is, the less liable it is to be disordered, and the easier repaired when disordered; and with this maxim in view, I offer a few remarks on the so much boasted constitution of England. That it was noble for the dark and slavish times in which it was erected, is granted. When the world was overrun with tyranny the least remove therefrom was a glorious rescue. But that it is imperfect, subject to convulsions, and incapable of producing what it seems to promise, is easily demonstrated.

Absolute governments (tho' the disgrace of human nature) have this advantage with them, that they are simple; if the people suffer, they know the head from which their suffering springs, know likewise the remedy, and are not bewildered by a variety of causes and cures. But the constitution of England is so exceedingly complex, that the nation may suffer for years together without being able to discover in which part the fault lies, some will say in one and some in another, and every political physician will advise a different medicine.

I know it is difficult to get over local or long standing prejudices, yet if we will suffer ourselves to examine the component parts of the English constitution, we shall find them to be the base remains of two ancient tyrannies, compounded with some new republican materials.

First. —The remains of monarchical tyranny in the person of the king.

Secondly. —The remains of aristocratical tyranny in the persons of the peers.

Thirdly. —The new republican materials, in the persons of the commons, on whose virtue depends the freedom of England.

The two first, by being hereditary, are independent of the people; wherefore in a constitutional sense they contribute nothing towards the freedom of the state.

To say that the constitution of England is a union of three powers reciprocally checking each other, is farcical, either the words have no meaning, or they are flat contradictions.

To say that the commons is a check upon the king, presupposes two things.

First. —That the king is not to be trusted without being

looked after, or in other words, that a thirst for absolute power is the natural disease of monarchy.

Secondly. —That the commons, by being appointed for that purpose, are either wiser or more worthy of confidence than the crown.

But as the same constitution which gives the commons a power to check the king by withholding the supplies, gives afterwards the king a power to check the commons, by empowering him to reject their other bills; it again supposes that the king is wiser than those whom it has already supposed to be wiser than him. A mere absurdity!

There is something exceedingly ridiculous in the composition of monarchy; it first excludes a man from the means of information, yet empowers him to act in cases where the highest judgment is required. The state of a king shuts him from the world, yet the business of a king requires him to know it thoroughly; wherefore the different parts, by unnaturally opposing and destroying each other, prove the whole character to be absurd and useless.

Some writers have explained the English constitution thus: The king, say they, is one, the people another; the peers are an house in behalf of the king; the commons in behalf of the people; but this hath all the distinctions of an house divided against itself; and though the expressions be pleasantly arranged, yet when examined they appear idle and ambiguous; and it will always happen, that the nicest construction that words are capable of, when applied to the description of some thing which either cannot exist, or is too incomprehensible to be within the compass of description, will be words of sound only, and though they may amuse the ear, they cannot inform the mind, for this explanation includes a previous question, viz. How came the king by a power which the people are afraid to trust, and always obliged to check? Such a power could not be the gift of a wise people, neither can any power, which needs checking, be from God; yet the provision, which the constitution makes, supposes such a power to exist.

But the provision is unequal to the task; the means either cannot or will not accomplish the end, and the whole affair is a felo de se; for as the greater weight will always carry up the less, and as all the wheels of a machine are put in motion by one, it only remains to know which power in the constitution has the most weight, for that will govern; and though the others, or a part of them, may clog, or, as the phrase is, check the rapidity of its motion, yet so long as they cannot stop it, their endeavors will be ineffectual; the first moving power will at last have its way, and what it wants in speed is supplied by time.

That the crown is this overbearing part in the English constitution needs not be mentioned, and that it derives its whole consequence merely from being the giver of places and pensions is self – evident; wherefore, though we have been wise enough to shut and lock a door against absolute monarchy, we at the same time have been foolish enough to put the crown in possession of the key.

The prejudice of Englishmen in favour of their own government by king, lords and commons, arises as much or more from national pride than reason. Individuals are undoubtedly safer in England than in some other countries, but the will of the king is as much the law of the land in Britain as in France, with this difference, that instead of proceeding directly from his mouth, it is handed to the people under the more formidable shape of an act of parliament. For the fate of Charles the First hath only made kings more subtle—not more just.

Wherefore, laying aside all national pride and prejudice in favour of modes and forms, the plain truth is, that it is wholly owing to the constitution of the people, and not to the constitution of the government that the crown is not as oppressive in England as in Turkey.

An inquiry into the constitutional errors in the English form of government is at this time highly necessary; for as we are never in a proper condition of doing justice to others, while we continue under the influence of some leading partiality, so neither are we capable of doing it to ourselves while we remain fettered by any

obstinate prejudice. And as a man, who is attached to a prosti-
tute, is unfitted to choose or judge of a wife, so any prepossession
in favour of a rotten constitution of government will disable us
from discerning a good one.

Of monarchy and hereditary succession

Mankind being originally equals in the order of creation, the equality could only be destroyed by some subsequent circumstance; the distinctions of rich, and poor, may in a great measure be accounted for, and that without having recourse to the harsh ill – sounding names of oppression and avarice. Oppression is often the consequence, but seldom or never the means of riches; and though avarice will preserve a man from being necessitously poor, it generally makes him too timorous to be wealthy.

But there is another and greater distinction for which no truly natural or religious reason can be assigned, and that is, the distinction of men into KINGS and SUBJECTS. Male and female are the distinctions of nature, good and bad the distinctions of heaven; but how a race of men came into the world so exalted above the rest, and distinguished like some new species, is worth enquiring into, and whether they are the means of happiness or of misery to mankind.

In the early ages of the world, according to the scripture chronology, there were no kings; the consequence of which was there were no wars; it is the pride of kings which throw mankind into confusion. Holland without a king hath enjoyed more peace for this last century than any of the monarchical governments in Europe. Antiquity favors the same remark; for the quiet and rural lives of the first patriarchs hath a happy something in them, which vanishes away when we come to the history of Jewish royalty.

Government by kings was first introduced into the world by the Heathens, from whom the children of Israel copied the custom. It was the most prosperous invention the Devil ever set on foot for the promotion of idolatry. The Heathens paid divine honors to their deceased kings, and the Christian world hath improved on the plan by doing the same to their living ones. How impious is the title of sacred majesty applied to a worm, who in the midst of his splendor is crumbling into dust!

As the exalting one man so greatly above the rest cannot be justified on the equal rights of nature, so neither can it be defended on the authority of scripture; for the will of the Almighty, as declared by Gideon and the prophet Samuel, expressly disapproves of government by kings. All antimonarchical parts of scripture have been very smoothly glossed over in monarchical governments, but they undoubtedly merit the attention of countries which have their governments yet to form. "Render unto Caesar the things which are Caesar's" is the scripture doctrine of courts, yet it is no support of monarchical government, for the Jews at that time were without a king, and in a state of vassalage to the Romans.

Near three thousand years passed away from the Mosaic account of the creation, till the Jews under a national delusion requested a king. Till then their form of government (except in extraordinary cases, where the Almighty interposed) was a kind of republic administered by a judge and the elders of the tribes. Kings they had none, and it was held sinful to acknowledge any being under that title but the Lord of Hosts. And when a man seriously reflects on the idolatrous homage which is paid to the persons of kings, he need not wonder that the Almighty ever jealous of his honor, should disapprove of a form of government which so impiously invades the prerogative of heaven.

Monarchy is ranked in scripture as one of the sins of the Jews, for which a curse in reserve is denounced against them. The history of that transaction is worth attending to.

The children of Israel being oppressed by the Midianites, Gideon marched against them with a small army, and victory, thro's the divine interposition, decided in his favour. The Jews elate with success, and attributing it to the generalship of Gideon, proposed making him a king, saying, Rule thou over us, thou and thy son and thy son's son. Here was temptation in its fullest extent; not a kingdom only, but an hereditary one, but Gideon in the piety of his soul replied, I will not rule over you, neither shall my son rule over you. THE LORD SHALL RULE OVER YOU. Words need not be more explicit; Gideon doth not decline the honor, but denieth their right to give it; neither doth he compliment them with invented declarations of his thanks, but in the positive stile of a prophet charges them with disaffection to their proper Sovereign, the King of heaven.

About one hundred and thirty years after this, they fell again into the same error. The hankering which the Jews had for the idolatrous customs of the Heathens, is something exceedingly unaccountable; but so it was, that laying hold of the misconduct of Samuel's two sons, who were entrusted with some secular concerns, they came in an abrupt and clamorous manner to Samuel, saying, Behold thou art old, and thy sons walk not in thy ways, now make us a king to judge us like all the other nations. And here we cannot but observe that their motives were bad, viz. that they might be like unto other nations, i. e. the Heathens, whereas their true glory laid in being as much unlike them as possible. But the thing displeased Samuel when they said, Give us a king to judge us; and Samuel prayed unto the Lord, and the Lord said unto Samuel, Hearken unto the voice of the people in all that they say unto thee, for they have not rejected thee, but they have rejected me, THAT I SHOULD NOT REIGN OVER THEM. According to all the works which they have done since the day that I brought them up out of Egypt, even unto this day; wherewith they have forsaken me and served other Gods; so do they also unto thee. Now therefore hearken unto their voice, howbeit, protest solemnly unto them and shew them the manner of the king that shall reign over them, i. e. not of any particular king, but the general manner of the kings of the earth, whom Israel was so eagerly copying after. And notwithstanding the great distance of time and difference of manners, the character is still in fashion. And Samuel told all the words of the Lord unto the people, that asked of him a king. And he said, This shall be the manner of the king that shall reign over you; he will take your sons and appoint them for himself, for his chariots, and to be his horsemen, and some shall run before his chariots (this description agrees with the present mode of impressing men) and he will appoint him captains over thousands and captains over fifties, and will set them to ear his ground and to read his harvest, and to make his instruments of war, and instruments of his chariots; and he will take your daughters to be confectionaries, and to be cooks and to be bakers (this describes the expence and luxury as well as the oppression of kings) and he will take your fields and your olive yards, even the best of them, and give them to his servants; and he will take the tenth of your seed, and of your vineyards, and give them to his officers and to his servants (by which we see that bribery, corruption, and favoritism are the standing vices of kings) and he will take the tenth of your men servants, and your maid servants, and your goodliest young men and your asses, and put them to his work; and he will take the tenth of your sheep, and ye shall be his servants, and ye shall cry out in that day because of your king which ye shall have chosen, AND THE LORD WILL NOT HEAR YOU IN THAT DAY. This accounts for the continuation of monarchy; neither do the characters of the few good kings which have lived since, either sanctify the title, or blot out the sinfulness of the origin; the high encomium given of David takes no notice of him officially as a king, but only as a man after God's own heart. Nevertheless the People refused to obey the voice of Samuel, and they said, Nay, but we will have a king over us, that we may be like all the nations, and that our king may judge us, and go out before us, and fight our battles. Samuel continued to reason with them, but to no purpose; he set before them their ingratitude, but all would not avail; and seeing them fully bent on their folly, he cried out, I will call unto the Lord, and he shall send thunder and rain (which then was a punishment, being in the time of wheat harvest) that ye may perceive and see that your wickedness is great which ye have done in the sight of the Lord, IN ASKING YOU A KING. So

Samuel called unto the Lord, and the Lord sent thunder and rain that day, and all the people greatly feared the Lord and Samuel. And all the people said unto Samuel, Pray for thy servants unto the Lord thy God that we die not, for WE HAVE ADDED UNTO OUR SINS THIS EVIL, TO ASK A KING. These portions of scripture are direct and positive. They admit of no equivocal construction. That the Almighty hath here entered his protest against monarchical government is true, or the scripture is false. And a man hath good reason to believe that there is as much of king – craft, as priest – craft, in withholding the scripture from the public in Popish countries. For monarchy in every instance is the Popery of government.

To the evil of monarchy we have added that of hereditary succession; and as the first is a degradation and lessening of ourselves, so the second, claimed as a matter of right, is an insult and an imposition on posterity. For all men being originally equals, no one by birth could have a right to set up his own family in perpetual preference to all others for ever, and though himself might deserve some decent degree of honors of his cotemporaries, yet his descendants might be far too unworthy to inherit them. One of the strongest natural proofs of the folly of hereditary right in kings, is, that nature disapproves it, otherwise, she would not so frequently turn it into ridicule by giving mankind an Ass for a Lion.

Secondly, as no man at first could possess any other public honors than were bestowed upon him, so the givers of those honors could have no power to give away the right of posterity. And though they might say "We choose you for our head," they could not, without manifest injustice to their children, say "that your children and your children's children shall reign over ours for ever." Because such an unwise, unjust, unnatural compact might (perhaps) in the next succession put them under the government of a rogue or a fool. Most wise men, in their private sentiments, have ever treated hereditary right with contempt; yet it is one of those evils, which when once established is not easily removed; many submit from fear, others from superstition, and the more powerful part shares with the king the plunder of the rest.

This is supposing the present race of kings in the world to have had an honorable origin; whereas it is more than probable, that could we take off the dark covering of antiquity, and trace them to their first rise, that we should find the first of them nothing better than the principal ruffian of some restless gang, whose savage manners or pre-eminence in subtility obtained him the title of chief among plunderers; and who by increasing in power, and extending his depredations, overawed the quiet and defenceless to purchase their safety by frequent contributions. Yet his electors could have no idea of giving hereditary right to his descendants, because such a perpetual exclusion of themselves was incompatible with the free and unrestrained principles they professed to live by. Wherefore, hereditary succession in the early ages of monarchy could not take place as a matter of claim, but as something casual or complimental; but as few or no records were extant in those days, and traditionary history stuffed with fables, it was very easy, after the lapse of a few generations, to trump up some superstitious tale, conveniently timed, Mahomet like, to cram hereditary right down the throats of the vulgar. Perhaps the disorders which threatened, or seemed to threaten, on the decease of a leader and the choice of a new one (for elections among ruffians could not be very orderly) induced many at first to favor hereditary pretensions; by which means it happened, as it hath happened since, that what at first was submitted to as a convenience, was afterwards claimed as a right.

England, since the conquest, hath known some few good monarchs, but groaned beneath a much larger number of bad ones; yet no man in his senses can say that their claim under William the Conqueror is a very honorable one. A French bastard landing with an armed banditti, and establishing himself king of England against the consent of the natives, is in plain terms a very paltry rascally original. —It certainly hath no divinity in it. However, it is needless to spend much time in exposing the folly of hereditary right, if there are any so weak as to believe it, let them promiscuously worship the ass and lion, and welcome. I shall neither copy their humility, nor disturb their devotion.

Yet I should be glad to ask how they suppose kings came at first? The question admits but of three answers, viz. either by lot, by election, or by usurpation. If the first king was taken by lot, it establishes a precedent for the next, which excludes hereditary succession. Saul was by lot, yet the succession was not hereditary, neither does it appear from that transaction there was any intention it ever should. If the first king of any country was by election, that likewise establishes a precedent for the next; for to say, that the right of all future generations is taken away, by the act of the first electors, in their choice not only of a king, but of a family of kings for ever, hath no parrallel in or out of scripture but the doctrine of original sin, which supposes the free will of all men lost in Adam; and from such comparison, and it will admit of no other, hereditary succession can derive no glory. For as in Adam all sinned, and as in the first electors all men obeyed; as in the one all mankind were subjected to Satan, and in the other to Sovereignty; as our innocence was lost in the first, and our authority in the last; and as both disable us from reassuming some former state and privilege, it unanswerably follows that original sin and hereditary succession are parallels. Dishonorable rank! Inglorious connexion! Yet the most subtile sophist cannot produce a juster simile.

As to usurpation, no man will be so hardy as to defend it; and that William the Conqueror was an usurper is a fact not to be contradicted. The plain truth is, that the antiquity of English monarchy will not bear looking into.

But it is not so much the absurdity as the evil of hereditary succession which concerns mankind. Did it ensure a race of good and wise men it would have the seal of divine authority, but as it opens a door to the foolish, the wicked, and the improper, it hath in it the nature of oppression. Men who look upon themselves born to reign, and others to obey, soon grow insolent; selected from the rest of mankind their minds are early poisoned by importance; and the world they act in differs so materially from the world at large, that they have but little opportunity of knowing its true interests, and when they succeed to the government are frequently the most ignorant and unfit of any throughout the dominions.

Another evil which attends hereditary succession is, that the throne is subject to be possessed by a minor at any age; all which time the regency, acting under the cover of a king, have every opportunity and inducement to betray their trust. The same national misfortune happens, when a king worn out with age and infirmity, enters the last stage of human weakness. In both these cases the public becomes a prey to every miscreant, who can tamper successfully with the follies either of age or infancy.

The most plausible plea, which hath ever been offered in favour of hereditary succession, is, that it preserves a nation from civil wars; and were this true, it would be weighty; whereas, it is the most barefaced falsity ever imposed upon mankind. The whole history of England disowns the fact. Thirty kings and two minors have reigned in that distracted kingdom since the conquest, in which time there have been (including the Revolution) no less than eight civil wars and nineteen rebellions. Wherefore instead of making for peace, it makes against it, and destroys the very foundation it seems to stand on.

The contest for monarchy and succession, between the houses of York and Lancaster, laid England in a scene of blood for many years. Twelve pitched battles, besides skirmishes and sieges, were fought between Henry and Edward. Twice was Henry prisoner to Edward, who in his turn was prisoner to Henry. And so uncertain is the fate of war and the temper of a nation, when nothing but personal matters are the ground of a quarrel, that Henry was taken in triumph from a prison to a palace, and Edward obliged to fly from a palace to a foreign land; yet, as sudden transitions of temper are seldom lasting, Henry in his turn was driven from the throne, and Edward recalled to succeed him. The parliament always following the strongest side.

This contest began in the reign of Henry the Sixth, and was not entirely extinguished till Henry the Seventh, in whom the families were united. Including a period of 67 years, viz. from 1422 to 1489.

In short, monarchy and succession have laid (not this or that kingdom only) but the world in blood and ashes. 'Tis a form of government which the word of God bears testimony against, and blood will attend it.

If we inquire into the business of a king, we shall find that in some countries they have none; and after sauntering away their lives without pleasure to themselves or advantage to the nation, withdraw from the scene, and leave their successors to tread the same idle ground. In absolute monarchies the whole weight of business, civil and military, lies on the king; the children of Israel in their request for a king, urged this plea "that he may judge us, and go out before us and fight our battles. " But in countries where he is neither a judge nor a general, as in England, a man would be puzzled to know what is his business.

The nearer any government approaches to a republic the less business there is for a king. It is somewhat difficult to find a proper name for the government of England. Sir William Meredith calls it a republic; but in its present state it is unworthy of the name, because the corrupt influence of the crown, by having all the places in its disposal, hath so effectually swallowed up the power, and eaten out the virtue of the house of commons (the republican part in the constitution) that the government of England is nearly as monarchical as that of France or Spain. Men fall out with names without understanding them. For it is the republican and not the monarchical part of the constitution of England which Englishmen glory in, viz. the liberty of choosing an house of commons from out of their own body—and it is easy to see that when republican virtue fails, slavery ensues. Why is the constitution of England sickly, but because monarchy hath poisoned the republic, the crown hath engrossed the commons?

In England a king hath little more to do than to make war and give away places; which in plain terms, is to impoverish the nation and set it together by the ears. A pretty business indeed for a man to be allowed eight hundred thousand sterling for a year, and worshipped into the bargain! Of more worth is one honest man to society and in the sight of God, than all the crowned ruffians that every lived.

Thoughts on the present state of American affairs

In the following pages I offer nothing more than simple facts, plain arguments, and common sense; and have no other preliminaries to settle with the reader, than that he will divest himself of prejudice and prepossession, and suffer his reason and his feelings to determine for themselves; that he will put on, or rather that he will not put off, the true character of a man, and generously enlarge his views beyond the present day.

Volumes have been written on the subject of the struggle between England and America. Men of all ranks have embarked in the controversy, from different motives, and with various designs; but all have been ineffectual, and the period of debate is closed. Arms, as the last resource, decide the contest; the appeal was the choice of the king, and the continent hath accepted the challenge.

It hath been reported of the late Mr. Pelham (who tho's an able minister was not without his faults) that on his being attacked in the house of commons, on the score, that his measures were only of a temporary kind, replied, "they will last my time." Should a thought so fatal and unmanly possess the colonies in the present contest, the name of ancestors will be remembered by future generations with detestation.

The sun never shined on a cause of greater worth. 'Tis not the affair of a city, a country, a province, or a kingdom, but of a continent—of at least one eighth part of the habitable globe. 'Tis not the concern of a day, a year, or an age; posterity are virtually involved in the contest, and will be more or less affected, even to the end of time, by the proceedings now. Now is the seed time of continental union, faith and honor. The least fracture now will be like a name engraved with the point of a pin on the tender rind of a young oak; the wound will enlarge with the tree, and posterity read it in full grown characters.

By referring the matter from argument to arms, a new aera for politics is struck; a new method of thinking hath arisen. All plans, proposals, & c. prior to the nineteenth of April, i. e. to the commencement of hostilities, are like the almanacks of the last year; which, though proper then, are superseded and useless now. Whatever was advanced by the advocates on either side of the question then, terminated in one and the same point, viz. a union with Great – Britain; the only difference between the parties was the method of effecting it; the one proposing force, the other friendship; but it hath so far happened that the first hath failed, and the second hath withdrawn her influence.

As much hath been said of the advantages of reconciliation, which, like an agreeable dream, hath passed away and left us as we were, it is but right, that we should examine the contrary side of the argument, and inquire into some of the many material injuries which these colonies sustain, and always will sustain, by being connected with, and dependant on Great – Britain. To examine that connexion and dependance, on the principles of nature and common sense, to see what we have to trust to, if separated, and what we are to expect, if dependant.

I have heard it asserted by some, that as America hath flourished under her former connexion with Great – Britain, that the same connexion is necessary towards her future happiness, and will always have the same effect. Nothing can be more fallacious than this kind of argument. We may as well assert that because a child has thrived upon milk, that it is never to have meat, or that the first twenty years of our lives is to become a precedent for the next twenty. But even this is admitting more than is true, for I answer roundly, that America would have flourished as much, and probably much more, had no European power had any thing to do with her. The commerce, by which she hath enriched herself are the necessaries of life, and will always have a market while eating is the custom of Europe.

But she has protected us, say some. That she has engrossed us is true, and defended the continent at our expence as well as her own is admitted, and she would have defended Turkey from the same motive, viz. the sake of trade and dominion.

Alas, we have been long led away by ancient prejudices, and made large sacrifices to superstition. We have boasted the protection of Great – Britain, without considering, that her motive was interest not attachment; that she did not protect us from our enemies on our account, but from her enemies on her own account, from those who had no quarrel with us on any other account, and who will always be our enemies on the same account. Let Britain waive her pretensions to the continent, or the continent throw off the dependance, and we should be at peace with France and Spain were they at war with Britain. The miseries of Hanover last war ought to warn us against connexions.

It hath lately been asserted in parliament, that the colonies have no relation to each other but through the parent country, i. e. that Pennsylvania and the Jerseys, and so on for the rest, are sister colonies by the way of England; this is certainly a very round – about way of proving relationship, but it is the nearest and only true way of proving enemyship, if I may so call it. France and Spain never were, nor perhaps ever will be our enemies as Americans, but as our being the subjects of Great – Britain.

But Britain is the parent country, say some. Then the more shame upon her conduct. Even brutes do not devour their young, nor savages make war upon their families; wherefore the assertion, if true, turns to her reproach; but it happens not to be true, or only partly so, and the phrase parent or mother country hath been jesuitically adopted by the king and his parasites, with a low papistical design of gaining an unfair bias on the credulous weakness of our minds. Europe, and not England, is the parent country of America. This new world hath been the asylum for the persecuted lovers of civil and religious liberty from every part of Europe. Hither have they fled, not from the tender embraces of the mother, but from the cruelty of the monster; and it is so far true of England, that the same tyranny which drove the first emigrants from home, pursues their descendants still.

In this extensive quarter of the globe, we forget the narrow limits of three hundred and sixty miles (the extent of England) and carry our friendship on a larger scale; we claim brotherhood with every European christian, and triumph in the generosity of the sentiment.

It is pleasant to observe by what regular gradations we surmount the force of local prejudice, as we enlarge our acquaintance with the world. A man born in any town in England divided into parishes, will naturally associate most with his fellow – parishioners (because their interests in many cases will be common) and distinguish him by the name of neighbour; if he meet him but a few miles from home, he drops the narrow idea of a street, and salutes him by the name of townsman; if he travel out of the county, and meet him in any other, he forgets the minor divisions of street and town, and calls him countryman; i. e. county – man; but if in their foreign excursions they should associate in France or any other part of Europe, their local remembrance would be enlarged into that of Englishmen. And by a just parity of reasoning, all Europeans meeting in America, or any other quarter of the globe, are countrymen; for England, Holland, Germany, or Sweden, when compared with the whole, stand in the same places on the larger scale, which the divisions of street, town, and county do on the smaller ones; distinctions too limited for continental minds. Not one third of the inhabitants, even of this province, are of English descent. Wherefore I reprobate the phrase of parent or mother country applied to England only, as being false, selfish, narrow and ungenerous.

But admitting, that we were all of English descent, what does it amount to? Nothing. Britain, being now an open enemy, extinguishes every other name and title: And to say that reconciliation is our duty, is truly farcical. The first king of England, of the present line (William the Conqueror) was a Frenchman, and half the Peers of England are descendants from the same country; wherefore, by the same method of reasoning, England ought to be governed by France.

Much hath been said of the united strength of Britain and the colonies, that in conjunction they might bid defiance to the world. But this is mere presumption; the fate of war is uncertain, neither do the expressions mean any thing; for this continent would never suffer itself to be drained of inhabitants, to support the British arms in either Asia, Africa, or Europe.

Besides, what have we to do with setting the world at defiance? Our plan is commerce, and that, well attended to, will secure us the peace and friendship of all Europe; because, it is the interest of all Europe to have America a free port. Her trade will always be a protection, and her barrenness of gold and silver secure her from invaders.

I challenge the warmest advocate for reconciliation, to shew, a single advantage that this continent can reap, by being connected with Great Britain. I repeat the challenge, not a single advantage is derived. Our corn will fetch its price in any market in Europe, and our imported goods must be paid for buy them where we will.

But the injuries and disadvantages we sustain by that connection, are without number; and our duty to mankind at large, as well as to ourselves, instruct us to renounce the alliance: Because, any submission to, or dependance on Great – Britain, tends directly to involve this continent in European wars and quarrels; and sets us at variance with nations, who would otherwise seek our friendship, and against whom, we have neither anger nor complaint. As Europe is our market for trade, we ought to form no partial connexion with any part of it. It is the true interest of America to steer clear of European contentions, which she never can do, while by her dependance on Britain, she is made the make – weight in the scale on British politics.

Europe is too thickly planted with kingdoms to be long at peace, and whenever a war breaks out between England and any foreign power, the trade of America goes to ruin, because of her connexion with Britain. The next war may not turn out like the last, and should it not, the advocates for reconciliation now will be wishing for separation then, because, neutrality in that case, would be a safer convoy than a man of war. Every thing that is right or natural pleads for separation. The blood of the slain, the weeping voice of nature cries, 'TIS TIME TO PART. Even the distance at which the Almighty hath placed England and America, is a strong and natural proof, that the authority of the one, over the other, was never the design of Heaven. The time likewise at which the continent was discovered, adds weight to the argument, and the manner in which it was peopled encreases the force of it. The reformation was preceded by the discovery of America, as if the Almighty graciously meant to open a sanctuary to the persecuted in future years, when home should afford neither friendship nor safety.

The authority of Great – Britain over this continent, is a form of government, which sooner or later must have an end: And a serious mind can draw no true pleasure by looking forward, under the painful and positive conviction, that what he calls "the present constitution" is merely temporary. As parents, we can have no joy, knowing that this government is not sufficiently lasting to ensure any thing which we may bequeath to posterity: And by a plain method of argument, as we are running the next generation into debt, we ought to do the work of it, otherwise we use them meanly and pitifully. In order to discover the line of our duty rightly, we should take our children in our hand, and fix our station a few years farther into life; that eminence will present a prospect, which a few present fears and prejudices conceal from our sight.

Though I would carefully avoid giving unnecessary offence, yet I am inclined to believe, that all those who espouse the doctrine of reconciliation, may be included within the following descriptions. Interested men, who are not to be trusted; weak men, who cannot see; prejudiced men, who will not see; and a certain set of moderate men, who think better of the European world than it deserves; and this last class, by an ill – judged deliberation, will be the cause of more calamities to this continent, than all the other three.

It is the good fortune of many to live distant from the scene of sorrow; the evil is not sufficiently brought to their doors to make them feel the precariousness with which all American property is possessed. But let our imaginations transport us for a few moments to Boston, that seat of wretchedness will teach us wisdom, and instruct us for ever to renounce a power in whom we can have no trust. The inhabitants of that unfortunate city, who but a few months ago were in ease and affluence, have now, no other alternative than to stay and starve, or turn out to beg. Endangered by the fire of their friends if they continue within the city, and plundered by the soldiery if they leave it. In their present condition they are prisoners without the hope of redemption, and in a general attack for their relief, they would be exposed to the fury of both armies.

Men of passive tempers look somewhat lightly over the offences of Britain, and, still hoping for the best, are apt to call out, "Come, come, we shall be friends again, for all this. " But examine the passions and feelings of mankind, bring the doctrine of reconciliation to the touchstone of nature, and then tell me, whether you can hereafter love, honour, and faithfully serve the power that hath carried fire and sword into your land? If you cannot do all these, then are you only deceiving yourselves, and by your delay bringing ruin upon posterity. Your future connexion with Britain, whom you can neither love nor honour, will be forced and unnatural, and being formed only on the plan of present convenience, will in a little time fall into a relapse more wretched than the first. But if you say, you can still pass the violations over, then I ask, Hath your house been burnt? Hath your property been destroyed before your face? Are your wife and children destitute of a bed to lie on, or bread to live on? Have you lost a parent or a child by their hands, and yourself the ruined and wretched survivor? If you have not, then are you not a judge of those who have. But if you have, and still can shake hands with the murderers, then you are unworthy of the name of husband, father, friend, or lover, and whatever may be your rank or title in life, you have the heart of a coward, and the spirit of a sycophant.

This is not inflaming or exaggerating matters, but trying them by those feelings and affections which nature justifies, and without which, we should be incapable of discharging the social duties of life, or enjoying the felicities of it. I mean not to exhibit horror for the purpose of provoking revenge, but to awaken us from fatal and unmanly slumbers, that we may pursue determinately some fixed object. It is not in the power of Britain or of Europe to conquer A- merica, if she do not conquer herself by delay and timidity. The present winter is worth an age if rightly employed, but if lost or neglected, the whole continent will partake of the misfortune; and there is no punishment which that man will not deserve, be he who, or what, or where he will, that may be the means of sacrifi- cing a season so precious and useful.

It is repugnant to reason, to the universal order of things to all examples from former ages, to suppose, that this continent can longer remain subject to any external power. The most sanguine in Britain does not think so. The utmost stretch of human wisdom cannot, at this time, compass a plan short of separation, which can promise the continent even a year's security. Reconciliation is now a fallacious dream. Nature hath deserted the connexion, and Art cannot supply her place. For, as Milton wisely expresses, "never can true reconcilement grow where wounds of deadly hate have pierced so deep. "

Every quiet method for peace hath been ineffectual. Our prayers have been rejected with disdain; and only tended to con- vince us, that nothing flatters vanity, or confirms obstinacy in Kings more than repeated petitioning—and noting hath contribu- ted more than that very measure to make the Kings of Europe absolute: Witness Denmark and Sweden. Wherefore, since nothing but blows will do, for God's sake, let us come to a final separation, and not leave the next generation to be cutting throats, under the violated unmeaning names of parent and child.

To say, they will never attempt it again is idle and visionary, we thought so at the repeal of the stamp act, yet a year or two undeceived us; as well may we suppose that nations, which have been once defeated, will never renew the quarrel.

As to government matters, it is not in the power of Britain to do this continent justice: The business of it will soon be too weighty, and intricate, to be managed with any tolerable degree of convenience, by a power, so distant from us, and so very ignorant of us; for if they cannot conquer us, they cannot govern us. To be always running three or four thousand miles with a tale or a petition, waiting four or five months for an answer, which when obtained requires five or six more to explain it in, will in a few years be looked upon as folly and childishness—There was a time when it was proper, and there is a proper time for it to cease.

Small islands not capable of protecting themselves, are the proper objects for kingdoms to take under their care; but there is something very absurd, in supposing a continent to be perpetually governed by an island. In no instance hath nature made the satellite larger than its primary planet, and as England and America, with respect to each other, reverses the common order of nature, it is evident they belong to different systems: England to Europe, America to itself.

I am not induced by motives of pride, party, or resentment to espouse the doctrine of separation and independance; I am clearly, positively, and conscientiously persuaded that it is the true interest of this continent to be so; that every thing short of that is mere patchwork, that it can afford no lasting felicity, —that it is leaving the sword to our children, and shrinking back at a time, when, a little more, a little farther, would have rendered this continent the glory of the earth.

As Britain hath not manifested the least inclination towards a compromise, we may be assured that no terms can be obtained worthy the acceptance of the continent, or any ways equal to the expense of blood and treasure we have been already put to.

The object, contended for, ought always to bear some just proportion to the expense. The removal of North, or the whole detestable junto, is a matter unworthy the millions we have expended. A temporary stoppage of trade, was an inconvenience, which would have sufficiently balanced the repeal of all the acts complained of, had such repeals been obtained; but if the whole continent must take up arms, if every man must be a soldier, it is scarcely worth our while to fight against a contemptible ministry only. Dearly, dearly, do we pay for the repeal of the acts, if that is all we fight for; for in a just estimation, it is as great a folly to pay a Bunker – hill price for law, as for land. As I have always considered the independancy of this continent, as an event, which sooner or later must arrive, so from the late rapid progress of the continent to maturity, the event could not be far off. Wherefore, on the breaking out of hostilities, it was not worth the while to have disputed a matter, which time would have finally redressed, unless we meant to be in earnest; otherwise, it is like wasting an estate on a suit at law, to regulate the trespasses of a tenant, whose lease is just expiring. No man was a warmer wisher for reconciliation than myself, before the fatal nineteenth of April 1775 [117], but the moment the event of that day was made known, I rejected the hardened, sullen tempered Pharaoh of England for ever; and disdain the wretch, that with the pretended title of FATHER OF HIS PEOPLE, can unfeelingly hear of their slaughter, and composedly sleep with their blood upon his soul.

But admitting that matters were now made up, what would be the event? I answer, the ruin of the continent. And that for several reasons.

First. The powers of governing still remaining in the hands of

---

[117] Massacre at Lexington.

the king, he will have a negative over the whole legislation of this continent. And as he hath shewn himself such an inveterate enemy to liberty, and discovered such a thirst for arbitrary power; is he, or is he not, a proper man to say to these colonies, "You shall make no laws but what I please." And is there any inhabitant in America so ignorant, as not to know, that according to what is called the present constitution, that this continent can make no laws but what the king gives it leave to; and is there any man so unwise, as not to see, that (considering what has happened) he will suffer no law to be made here, but such as suit his purpose. We may be as effectually enslaved by the want of laws in America, as by submitting to laws made for us in England. After matters are made up (as it is called) can there be any doubt, but the whole power of the crown will be exerted, to keep this continent as low and humble as possible? Instead of going forward we shall go backward, or be perpetually quarrelling or ridiculously petitioning. We are already greater than the king wishes us to be, and will he not hereafter endeavour to make us less? To bring the matter to one point. Is the power who is jealous of our prosperity, a proper power to govern us? Whoever says No to this question is an independant, for independancy means no more, than, whether we shall make our own laws, or, whether the king, the greatest enemy this continent hath, or can have, shall tell us, "there shall be no laws but such as I like. "

But the king you will say has a negative in England; the people there can make no laws without his consent. In point of right and good order, there is something very ridiculous, that a youth of twenty – one (which hath often happened) shall say to several millions of people, older and wiser than himself, I forbid this or that act of yours to be law. But in this place I decline this sort of reply, though I will never cease to expose the absurdity of it, and only answer, that England being the King's residence, and America not so, make quite another case. The king's negative here is ten times more dangerous and fatal than it can be in England, for there he will scarcely refuse his consent to a bill for putting England into as strong a state of defence as possible, and in America he would never suffer such a bill to be passed.

America is only a secondary object in the system of British politics, England consults the good of this country, no farther than it answers her own purpose. Wherefore, her own interest leads her to suppress the growth of ours in every case which doth not promote her advantage, or in the least interferes with it. A pretty state we should soon be in under such a second – hand government, considering what has happened! Men do not change from enemies to friends by the alteration of a name: And in order to shew that reconciliation now is a dangerous doctrine, I affirm, that it would be policy in the king at this time, to repeal the acts for the sake of reinstating himself in the government of the provinces; in order that HE MAY ACCOMPLISH BY CRAFT AND SUBTILITY, IN THE LONG RUN, WHAT HE CANNOT DO BY FORCE AND VIOLENCE IN THE SHORT ONE. Reconciliation and ruin are nearly related.

Secondly. That as even the best terms, which we can expect to obtain, can amount to no more than a temporary expedient, or a kind of government by guardianship, which can last no longer than till the colonies come of age, so the general face and state of things, in the interim, will be unsettled and unpromising. Emigrants of property will not choose to come to a country whose form of government hangs but by a thread, and who is every day tottering on the brink of commotion and disturbance; and numbers of the present inhabitants would lay hold of the interval, to dispose of their effects, and quit the continent.

But the most powerful of all arguments, is, that nothing but independance, i. e. a continental form of government, can keep the peace of the continent and preserve it inviolate from civil wars. I dread the event of a reconciliation with Britain now, as it is more than probable, that it will followed by a revolt somewhere or other, the consequences of which may be far more fatal than all the malice of Britain.

Thousands are already ruined by British barbarity; (thousands more will probably suffer the same fate.) Those men have other feelings than us who have nothing suffered. All they now possess is liberty, what they before enjoyed is sacrificed to its service, and having nothing more to lose, they disdain submission. Besides, the general temper of the colonies, towards a British government, will be like that of a youth, who is nearly out of his time; they will care very little about her. And a government which cannot preserve the peace, is no government at all, and in that case we pay our money for nothing; and pray what is it that Britain can do, whose power will be wholly on paper, should a civil tumult break out the very day after reconciliation? I have heard some men say, many of whom I believe spoke without thinking, that they dreaded an independance, fearing that it would produce civil wars. It is but seldom that our first thoughts are truly correct, and that is the case here; for there are ten times more to dread from a patched up connexion than from independance. I make the sufferers case my own, and I protest, that were I driven from house and home, my property destroyed, and my circumstances ruined, that as a man, sensible of injuries, I could never relish the doctrine of reconciliation, or consider myself bound thereby.

The colonies have manifested such a spirit of good order and obedience to continental government, as is sufficient to make every reasonable person easy and happy on that head. No man can assign the least pretence for his fears, on any other grounds, that such as are truly childish and ridiculous, viz. that one colony will be striving for superiority over another.

Where there are no distinctions there can be no superiority, perfect equality affords no temptation. The republics of Europe are all (and we may say always) in peace. Holland and Swisserland are without wars, foreign or domestic: Monarchical governments, it is true, are never long at rest; the crown itself is a temptation to enterprizing ruffians at home; and that degree of pride and insolence ever attendant on regal authority, swells into a rupture with foreign powers, in instances, where a republican government, by being formed on more natural principles, would negotiate the mistake.

If there is any true cause of fear respecting independance, it is because no plan is yet laid down. Men do not see their way out—Wherefore, as an opening into that business, I offer the following hints; at the same time modestly affirming, that I have no other opinion of them myself, than that they may be the means of giving rise to something better. Could the straggling thoughts of individuals be collected, they would frequently form materials for wise and able men to improve into useful matter.

Let the assemblies be annual, with a President only. The

representation more equal. Their business wholly domestic, and subject to the authority of a Continental Congress.

Let each colony be divided into six, eight, or ten, convenient districts, each district to send a proper number of delegates to Congress, so that each colony send at least thirty. The whole number in Congress will be least 390. Each Congress to sit and to choose a president by the following method. When the delegates are met, let a colony be taken from the whole thirteen colonies by lot, after which, let the whole Congress choose (by ballot) a president from out of the delegates of that province. In the next Congress, let a colony be taken by lot from twelve only, omitting that colony from which the president was taken in the former Congress, and so proceeding on till the whole thirteen shall have had their proper rotation. And in order that nothing may pass into a law but what is satisfactorily just, not less than three fifths of the Congress to be called a majority. —He that will promote discord, under a government so equally formed as this, would have joined Lucifer in his revolt.

But as there is a peculiar delicacy, from whom, or in what manner, this business must first arise, and as it seems most agreeable and consistent that it should come from some intermediate body between the governed andthe governors, that is, between the Congress and the people, let a CONTINENTAL CONFER-

ENCE be held, in the following manner, and for the following purpose.

A committee of twenty – six members of Congress, viz. two for each colony. Two members for each House of Assembly, or Provincial Convention; and five representatives of the people at large, to be chosen in the capital city or town of each province, for, and in behalf of the whole province, by as many qualified voters as shall think proper to attend from all parts of the province for that purpose; or, if more convenient, the representatives may be chosen in two or three of the most populous parts thereof. In this conference, thus assembled, will be united, the two grand principles of business, knowledge and power. The members of Congress, Assemblies, or Conventions, by having had experience in national concerns, will be able and useful counsellors, and the whole, being empowered by the people, will have a truly legal authority.

The conferring members being met, let their business be to frame a CONTINENTAL CHARTER, or Charter of the United Colonies; (answering to what is called the Magna Charta of England) fixing the number and manner of choosing members of Congress, members of Assembly, with their date of sitting, and drawing the line of business and jurisdiction between them: (Always remembering, that our strength is continental, not provincial:)

Securing freedom and property to all men, and above all things, the free exercise of religion, according to the dictates of conscience; with such other matter as is necessary for a charter to contain. Immediately after which, the said Conference to dissolve, and the bodies which shall be chosen comfortable to the said charter, to be the legislators and governors of this continent for the time being: Whose peace and happiness, may God preserve, Amen.

Should any body of men be hereafter delegated for this or some similar purpose, I offer them the following extracts from that wise observer on governments Dragonetti. "The science" says he "of the politician consists in fixing the true point of happiness and freedom. Those men would deserve the gratitude of ages, who should discover a mode of government that contained the greatest sum of individual happiness, with the least national expense. "

"Dragonetti on virtue and rewards. "

But where says some, is the King of America? I'll tell you Friend, he reigns above, and doth not make havoc of mankind like the Royal Brute of Britain. Yet that we may not appear to be defective even in earthly honors, let a day be solemnly set apart for proclaiming the charter; let it be brought forth placed on the divine law, the word of God; let a crown be placed thereon, by which the world may know, that so far as we approve as monarchy, that in America THE LAW IS KING. For as in absolute governments the King is law, so in free countries the law ought to be King; and there ought to be no other. But lest any ill use should afterwards arise, let the crown at the conclusion of the ceremony be demolished, and scattered among the people whose right it is.

A government of our own is our natural right: And when a man seriously reflects on the precariousness of human affairs, he will become convinced, that it is infinitely wiser and safer, to form a constitution of our own in a cool deliberate manner, while we have it in our power, than to trust such an interesting event to time and chance. If we omit it now, some, [118] Massanello may hereafter arise, who laying hold of popular disquietudes, may collect together the desperate and discontented, and by assuming to themselves the powers of government, may sweep away the liberties of the continent like a deluge. Should the government of America return again into the hands of Britain, the tottering situation of things, will be a temptation for some desperate adventurer to try his fortune; and in such a case, what relief can Britain give? Ere she could hear the news, the fatal business might be done; and ourselves suffering like the wretched Britons under the

---

[118] Thomas Anello, otherwise Massanello, a fisherman of Naples, who after spiriting up his countrymen in the public market place, against the oppression of the Spaniards, to whom the place was then subject, prompted them to revolt, and in the space of a day became king.

oppression of the Conqueror. Ye that oppose independance now, ye know not what ye do; ye are opening a door to eternal tyranny, by keeping vacant the seat of government. There are thousands, and tens of thousands, who would think it glorious to expel from the continent, that barbarous and hellish power, which hath stirred up the Indians and Negroes to destroy us; the cruelty hath a double guilt, it is dealing brutally by us, and treacherously by them.

To talk of friendship with those in whom our reason forbids us to have faith, and our affections wounded through a thousand pores instruct us to detest, is madness and folly. Every day wears out the little remains of kindred between us and them, and can there be any reason to hope, that as the relationship expires, the affection will increase, or that we shall agree better, when we have ten times more and greater concerns to quarrel over than ever?

Ye that tell us of harmony and reconciliation, can ye restore to us the time that is past? Can ye give to prostitution its former innocence? Neither can ye reconcile Britain and America. The last cord now is broken, the people of England are presenting addresses against us. There are injuries which nature cannot forgive; she would cease to be nature if she did. As well can the lover forgive the ravisher of his mistress, as the continent forgive the murders

of Britain. The Almighty hath implanted in us these unextinguish-
able feelings for good and wise purposes. They are the guardians of
his image in our hearts. They distinguish us from the herd of common animals. The social compact would dissolve, and justice be
extirpated the earth, or have only a casual existence were we cal-
lous to the touches of affection. The robber, and the murderer,
would often escape unpunished, did not the injuries which our
tempers sustain, provoke us into justice.

O ye that love mankind! Ye that dare oppose, not only the
tyranny, but the tyrant, stand forth! Every spot of the old world is
overrun with oppression. Freedom hath been hunted round the
globe. Asia, and Africa, have long expelled her. —Europe re-
gards her like a stranger, and England hath given her warning to
depart. O! receive the fugitive, and prepare in time an asylum for
mankind.

Of the present ability of America, with some miscellaneous reflexions

I HAVE never met with a man, either in England or America, who hath not confessed his opinion, that a separation between the countries, would take place one time or other: And there is no instance, in which we have shewn less judgment, than in endeavouring to describe, what we call, the ripeness or fitness of the Continent for independance.

As all men allow the measure, and vary only in their opinion of the time, let us, in order to remove mistakes, take a general survey of things, and endeavour, if possible, to find out the very time. But we need not go far, the inquiry ceases at once, for, the time hath found us. The general concurrence, the glorious union of all things prove the fact.

It is not in numbers, but in unity, that our great strength lies; yet our present numbers are sufficient to repel the force of all the world. The Continent hath, at this time, the largest body of armed and disciplined men of any power under Heaven; and is just arrived at that pitch of strength, in which, no single colony is able to support itself, and the whole, when united, can accomplish the matter, and either more, or, less than this, might be fatal in its effects. Our land force is already sufficient, and as to naval affairs, we cannot be insensible, that Britain would never suffer an American man of war to be built, while the continent remained in her hands. Wherefore, we should be no forwarder an hundred years hence in that branch, than we are now; but the truth is, we should be less so, because the timber of the country is every day diminishing, and that, which will remain at last, will be far off and difficult to procure.

Were the continent crowded with inhabitants, her sufferings under the present circumstances would be intolerable. The more seaport towns we had, the more should we have both to defend and to lose. Our present numbers are so happily proportioned to our wants, that no man need be idle. The diminution of trade affords an army, and the necessities of an army create a new trade.

Debts we have none; and whatever we may contract on this account will serve as a glorious memento of our virtue. Can we but leave posterity with a settled form of government, an independant constitution of its own, the purchase at any price will be cheap. But to expend millions for the sake of getting a few vile acts repealed, and routing the present ministry only, is unworthy the charge, and is using posterity with the utmost cruelty; because it is leaving them the great work to do, and a debt upon their backs, from which, they derive no advantage. Such a thought is unworthy a man of honor, and is the true characteristic of a narrow heart and a peddling politician.

The debt we may contract doth not deserve our regard if the work be but accomplished. No nation ought to be without a debt. A national debt is a national bond; and when it bears no interest, is in no case a grievance. Britain is oppressed with a debt of upwards of one hundred and forty millions sterling, for which she pays upwards of four millions interest. And as a compensation for her debt, she has a large navy; America is without a debt, and without a navy; yet for the twentieth part of the English national debt, could have a navy as large again. The navy of England is not worth, at this time, more than three millions and an half sterling.

The first and second editions of this pamphlet were published without the following calculations, which are now given as a proof that the above estimation of the navy is a just one. See Entic's naval history, intro. page 56.

The charge of building a ship of each rate, and furnishing her with masts, yards, sails and rigging, together with a proportion of eight months boatswain's and carpenter's sea – stores, as calculated by Mr. Burchett, Secretary to the navy.

	£.
For a ship of a 100 guns –	35,553
90	29,886
80	23,638
70	17,785
60	14,197
50	10,606
40	7,558
30	5,846
20	3,710

And from hence it is easy to sum up the value, or cost rather, of the whole British navy, which in the year 1757, when it was as its greatest glory consisted of the following ships and guns:

Ships.	Guns.	Cost of one.	Cost of all.
6	100	35,553 l.	213,318 l.
12	90	29,886	358,632
12	80	23,638	283,656
43	70	17,785	764,755
35	60	14,197	496,895
40	50	10,606	424,240
45	40	7,558	340,110
58	20	3,710	215,180

| 85 | Sloops, bombs, and fireships, one with another, 2,000 | 170,000 |

| | Cost 3,266,786 |
| Remains for guns | 233,214 |

3,500,000

No country on the globe is so happily situated, so internally capable of raising a fleet as America. Tar, timber, iron, and cordage are her natural produce. We need go abroad for nothing. Whereas the Dutch, who make large profits by hiring out their ships of war to the Spaniards and Portuguese, are obliged to import most of the materials they use. We ought to view the building a fleet as an article of commerce, it being the natural manufactory of this country. It is the best money we can lay out. A navy when finished is worth more than it cost. And is that nice point in national policy, in which commerce and protection are united. Let us build; if we want them not, we can sell; and by that means replace our paper currency with ready gold and silver.

In point of manning a fleet, people in general run into great errors; it is not necessary that one fourth part should be sailor. The Terrible privateer, Captain Death, stood the hottest engagement of any ship last war, yet had not twenty sailors on board, though her complement of men was upwards of two hundred. A few able and social sailors will soon instruct a sufficient number of active landmen in the common work of a ship. Wherefore, we never can be more capable to begin on maritime matters than now, while our timber is standing, our fisheries blocked up, and our sailors and shipwrights out of employ. Men of war of seventy and eighty guns were built forty years ago in New – England, and why not the same now? Ship – building is America's greatest pride, and in which, she will in time excel the whole world. The great empires of the east are mostly inland, and consequently excluded from the possibility of rivalling her. Africa is in a state of barbarism; and no power in Europe, hath either such an extent of coast, or such an internal supply of materials. Where nature hath given the one, she has withheld the other; to America only hath she been liberal of both. The vast empire of Russia is almost shut out from the sea: wherefore, her boundless forests, her tar, iron, and cordage are only articles of commerce.

In point of safety, ought we to be without a fleet? We are not the little people now, which we were sixty years ago; at that time we might have trusted our property in the streets, or fields rather; and slept securely without locks or bolts to our doors or windows. The case now is altered, and our methods of defence, ought to improve with our increase of property. A common pirate, twelve months ago, might have come up the Delaware, and laid the city of Philadelphia under instant contribution, for what sum he pleased; and the same might have happened to other places. Nay, any daring fellow, in a brig of fourteen or sixteen guns, might have robbed the whole Continent, and carried off half a million of money. These are circumstances which demand our attention, and point out the necessity of naval protection.

Some, perhaps, will say, that after we have made it up with Britain, she will protect us. Can we be so unwise as to mean, that she shall keep a navy in our harbours for that purpose? Common sense will tell us, that the power which hath endeavoured to subdue us, is of all others, the most improper to defend us. Conquest may be effected under the pretence of friendship; and ourselves, after a long and brave resistance, be at last cheated into slavery. And if her ships are not to be admitted into our harbours, I would ask, how is she to protect us? A navy three or four thousand miles off can be of little use, and on sudden emergencies, none at all. Wherefore, if we must hereafter protect ourselves, why not do it for ourselves? Why do it for another?

The English list of ships of war, is long and formidable, but not a tenth part of them are at any time fit for service, numbers of them not in being; yet their names are pompously continued in the list, if only a plank be left of the ship: and not a fifth part, of such as are fit for service, can be spared on any one station at one time. The East, and West Indies, Mediterranean, Africa, and other parts over which Britain extends her claim, make large demands upon her navy. From a mixture of prejudice and inattention, we have contracted a false notion respecting the navy of England, and have talked as if we should have the whole of it to encounter at once, and for that reason, supposed, that we must have one as large; which not being instantly practicable, have been made use of by a set of disguised Tories to discourage our beginning thereon. Nothing can be farther from truth than this; for if America had only a twentieth part of the naval force of Britain, she would be by far an overmatch for her; because, as we neither have, nor claim any foreign dominion, our whole force would be employed on our own coast, where we should, in the long run, have two to one the advantage of those who had three or four thousand miles to sail over, before they could attack us, and the same distance to return in order to refit and recruit. And although Britain by her fleet, hath a check over our trade to Europe, we have as large a one over her trade to the West – Indies, which, by laying in the neighbourhood of the Continent, is entirely at its mercy.

Some method might be fallen on to keep up a naval force in

time of peace, if we should not judge it necessary to support a constant navy. If premiums were to be given to merchants, to build and employ in their service, ships mounted with twenty, thirty, or fifty guns, (the premiums to be in proportion to the loss of bulk to the merchants) fifty or sixty of those ships, with a few guard ships on constant duty, would keep up a sufficient navy, and that without burdening ourselves with the evil so loudly complained of in England, of suffering their fleet, in time of peace to lie rotting in the docks. To unite the sinews of commerce and defence is sound policy; for when our strength and our riches, play into each other's hand, we need fear no external enemy.

In almost every article of defence we abound. Hemp flourishes even to rankness, so that we need not want cordage. Our iron is superior to that of other countries. Our small arms equal to any in the world. Cannons we can cast at pleasure. Saltpetre and gunpowder we are every day producing. Our knowledge is hourly improving. Resolution is our inherent character, and courage hath never yet forsaken us. Wherefore, what is it that we want? Why is it that we hesitate? From Britain we can expect nothing but ruin. If she is once admitted to the government of America again, this Continent will not be worth living in. Jealousies will be always arising; insurrections will be constantly happening; and who will go forth to quell them? Who will venture his life to reduce his own countrymen to a foreign obedience? The difference between Pennsylvania and Connecticut, respecting some unlocated lands, shews the insignificance of a British government, and fully proves, that nothing but Continental authority can regulate Continental matters.

Another reason why the present time is preferable to all others, is, that the fewer our numbers are, the more land there is yet unoccupied, which instead of being lavished by the king on his worthless dependents, may be hereafter applied, not only to the discharge of the present debt, but to the constant support of government. No nation under heaven hath such an advantage as this.

The infant state of the Colonies, as it is called, so far from being against, is an argument in favor of independance. We are sufficiently numerous, and were we more so, we might be less united. It is a matter worthy of observation, that the more a country is peopled, the smaller their armies are. In military numbers, the ancients far exceeded the moderns: and the reason is evident, for trade being the consequence of population, men become too much absorbed thereby to attend to anything else. Commerce diminishes the spirit, both of patriotism and military defence. And history sufficiently informs us, that the bravest achievements were always accomplished in the non – age of a nation. With the increase of commerce, England hath lost its spirit. The city of London, notwithstanding its numbers, submits to continued insults with the patience of a coward. The more men have to lose, the less willing are they to venture. The rich are in general slaves to fear, and submit to courtly power with the trembling duplicity of a Spaniel.

Youth is the seed time of good habits, as well in nations as in individuals. It might be difficult, if not impossible, to form the Continent into one government half a century hence. The vast variety of interests, occasioned by an increase of trade and population, would create confusion. Colony would be against colony. Each being able might scorn each other's assistance; and while the proud and foolish gloried in their little distinctions, the wise would lament, that the union had not been formed before. Wherefore, the present time is the true time for establishing it. The intimacy which is contracted in infancy, and the friendship which is formed in misfortune, are, of all others, the most lasting and unalterable. Our present union is marked with both these characters: we are young, and we have been distressed; but our concord hath withstood our troubles, and fixes a memorable area for posterity to glory in.

The present time, likewise, is that peculiar time, which never happens to a nation but once, viz. the time of forming itself into a government. Most nations have let slip the opportunity, and by that means have been compelled to receive laws from their conquerors, instead of making laws for themselves. First, they had a king, and then a form of government; whereas, the articles or charter of government, should be formed first, and men delegated to execute them afterwards: but from the errors of other nations, let us learn wisdom, and lay hold of the present opportunity—To begin government at the right end.

When William the Conqueror subdued England, he gave them law at the point of the sword; and until we consent, that the seat of government, in America, be legally and authoritatively occupied, we shall be in danger of having it filled by some fortunate ruffian, who may treat us in the same manner, and then, where will be our freedom? Where our property?

As to religion, I hold it to be the indispensible duty of all government, to protect all conscientious professors thereof, and I know of no other business which government hath to do therewith. Let a man throw aside that narrowness of soul, that selfishness of principle, which the niggards of all professions are so unwilling to part with, and he will be at once delivered of his fears on that head. Suspicion is the companion of mean souls, and the bane of all good society. For myself, I fully and conscientiously believe, that it is the will of the Almighty, that there should be diversity of religious opinions among us: It affords a larger field for our Christian kindness. Were we all of one way of thinking, our religious dispositions would want matter for probation; and on this liberal principle, I look on the various denominations among us, to be like children of the same family, differing only, in what is called, their Christian names.

In page [section Ⅲ, paragraph 47], I threw out a few thoughts on the propriety of a Continental Charter, (for I only presume to offer hints, not plans) and in this place, I take the liberty of rementioning the subject, by observing, that a charter is to be understood as a bond of solemn obligation, which the whole enters into, to support the right of every separate part, whether of religion, personal freedom, or property. A firm bargain and a right reckoning make long friends.

In a former page I likewise mentioned the necessity of a large and equal representation; and there is no political matter which more deserves our attention. A small number of electors, or a small number of representatives, are equally dangerous. But if the number of the representatives be not only small, but unequal, the danger is increased. As an instance of this, I mention the following; when the Associators petition was before the House of Assembly of Pennsylvania; twenty – eight members only were present, all the Bucks county members, being eight, voted against it, and had seven of the Chester members done the same, this whole province had been governed by two counties only, and this danger it is always exposed to. The unwarrantable stretch likewise, which that house made in their last sitting, to gain an undue authority over the Delegates of that province, ought to warn the people at large, how they trust power out of their own hands. A set of instructions for the Delegates were put together, which in point of sense and business would have dishonored a schoolboy, and after being approved by a few, a very few without doors, were carried into the House, and there passed in behalf of the whole colony; whereas, did the whole colony know, with what ill – will that House hath entered on some necessary public measures, they would not hesitate a moment to think them unworthy of such a trust.

Immediate necessity makes many things convenient, which if continued would grow into oppressions. Expedience and right are different things. When the calamities of America required a consultation, there was no method so ready, or at that time so proper, as to appoint persons from the several Houses of Assembly for that purpose; and the wisdom with which they have proceeded hath preserved this continent from ruin. But as it is more than probable that we shall never be without a CONGRESS, every well wisher to good order, must own, that the mode for choosing members of that body, deserves consideration. And I put it as a question to those, who make a study of mankind, whether representation and election is not too great a power for one and the same body of men to possess? When we are planning for posterity, we ought to remember, that virtue is not hereditary.

It is from our enemies that we often gain excellent maxims, and are frequently surprised into reason by their mistakes. Mr. Cornwall (one of the Lords of the Treasury) treated the petition of the New – York Assembly with contempt, because that House, he said, consisted but of twenty – six members, which trifling number, he argued, could not with decency be put for the whole. We thank him for his involuntary honesty. [119]

TO CONCLUDE, however strange it may appear to some, or however unwilling they may be to think so, matters not, but many strong and striking reasons may be given, to shew, that nothing can settle our affairs so expeditiously as an open and determined declaration for independance. Some of which are,

First. —It is the custom of nations, when any two are at war, for some other powers, not engaged in the quarrel, to step in as mediators, and bring about the preliminaries of a peace: but while America calls herself the Subject of Great – Britain, no power, however well disposed she may be, can offer her mediation. Wherefore, in our present state we may quarrel on for ever.

---

[119] Those who would fully understand of what great consequence a large and e-qual representation is to a state, should read Burgh's political Disquisitions.

Secondly. —It is unreasonable to suppose, that France or Spain will give us any kind of assistance, if we mean only, to make use of that assistance for the purpose of repairing the breach, and strengthening the connexion between Britain and America; because, those powers would be sufferers by the consequences.

Thirdly. —While we profess ourselves the subjects of Britain, we must, in the eye of foreign nations, be considered as rebels. The precedent is somewhat dangerous to their peace, for men to be in arms under the name of subjects; we, on the spot, can solve the paradox: but to unite resistance and subjection, requires an idea much too refined for the common understanding.

Fourthly. —Were a manifesto to be published, and despatched to foreign courts, setting forth the miseries we have endured, and the peaceable methods we have ineffectually used for redress; declaring, at the same time, that not being able, any longer, to live happily or safely under the cruel disposition of the British court, we had been driven to the necessity of breaking off all connections with her; at the same time, assuring all such courts of our peacable disposition towards them, and of our desire of entering into trade with them: Such a memorial would produce more good effects to this Continent, than if a ship were freighted with petitions to Britain.

Under our present denomination of British subjects, we can

neither be received nor heard abroad: The custom of all courts is against us, and will be so, until, by an independance, we take rank with other nations.

These proceedings may at first appear strange and difficult; but, like all other steps which we have already passed over, will in a little time become familiar and agreeable; and, until an independance is declared, the Continent will feel itself like a man who continues putting off some unpleasant business from day to day, yet knows it must be done, hates to set about it, wishes it over, and is continually haunted with the thoughts of its necessity.

Appendix

SINCE the publication of the first edition of this pamphlet, or rather, on the same day on which it came out, the King's Speech made its appearance in this city. Had the spirit of prophecy directed the birth of this production, it could not have brought it forth, at a more seasonable juncture, or a more necessary time. The bloody mindedness of the one, shew the necessity of pursuing the doctrine of the other. Men read by way of revenge.
And the Speech instead of terrifying, prepared a way for the manly principles of Independance.

Ceremony, and even, silence, from whatever motive they may arise, have a hurtful tendency, when they give the least degree of countenance to base and wicked performances; wherefore, if this maxim be admitted, it naturally follows, that the King's Speech, as being a piece of finished villainy, deserved, and still deserves, a general execration both by the Congress and the people. Yet, as the domestic tranquillity of a nation, depends greatly, on the chastity of what may properly be called NATIONAL MANNERS, it is often better, to pass some things over in silent disdain, than to make use of such new methods of dislike, as might introduce the least innovation, on that guardian of our peace and safety. And, perhaps, it is chiefly owing to this prudent delicacy, that the King's Speech, hath not, before now, suffered a public execution. The Speech if it may be called one, is nothing better than a wilful audacious libel against the truth, the common good, and the existence of mankind; and is a formal and pompous method of offering up human sacrifices to the pride of tyrants. But this general massacre of mankind, is one of the privileges, and the certain consequence of Kings; for as nature knows them not, they know not her, and although they are beings of our own creating, they know not us, and are become the gods of their creators. The Speech hath one good quality, which is, that it is not calculated to deceive, neither can we, even if we would, be deceived by it. Brutality and tyranny appear on the face of it. It leaves us at no loss: And every line convinces, even in the moment of reading, that He, who hunts the woods for prey, the naked and untutored Indian, is less a Savage than the King of Britain.

Sir John Dalrymple, the putative father of a whining Jesuitical piece, fallaciously called, " The Address of the people of ENGLAND to the inhabitants of AMERICA," hath, perhaps, from a vain supposition, that the people here were to be frightened at the pomp and description of a king, given, (though very unwisely on his part) the real character of the present one: "But," says this writer, "if you are inclined to pay compliments to an administration, which we do not complain of," (meaning the Marquis of Rockingham's at the repeal of the Stamp Act) "it is very unfair in you to withhold them from that prince, by whose NOD ALONE they were permitted to do anything." This is toryism with a witness! Here is idolatry even without a mask: And he who can so calmly hear, and digest such doctrine, hath forfeited his claim to rationality—an apostate from the order of manhood; and ought to be considered—as one, who hath, not only given up the proper dignity of a man, but sunk himself beneath the rank of animals, and contemptibly crawl through the world like a worm.

However, it matters very little now, what the king of England either says or does; he hath wickedly broken through every moral and human obligation, trampled nature and conscience beneath his feet; and by a steady and constitutional spirit of insolence and cruelty, procured for himself an universal hatred. It is now the interest of America to provide for herself. She hath already a large and young family, whom it is more her duty to take care of, than to be granting away her property, to support a power who is become a reproach to the names of men and Christians—YE, whose office it is to watch over the morals of a nation, of whatsoever sect or denomination ye are of, as well as ye, who, are more immediately the guardians of the public liberty, if ye wish to pre-serve your native country uncontaminated by European corruption, ye must in secret wish a separation—But leaving the moral part to private reflection, I shall chiefly confine my farther remarks to the following heads.

First. That it is the interest of America to be separated from Britain.

Secondly. Which is the easiest and most practicable plan, RECONCILIATION or INDEPENDANCE? with some occasional remarks.

In support of the first, I could, if I judged it proper, produce the opinion of some of the ablest and most experienced men on this continent; and whose sentiments, on that head, are not yet publicly known. It is in reality a self – evident position: For no nation in a state of foreign dependance, limited in its commerce, and cramped and fettered in its legislative powers, can ever arrive at any material eminence. America doth not yet know what opu-lence is; and although the progress which she hath made stands unparalleled in the history of other nations, it is but childhood, compared with what she would be capable of arriving at, had she, as she ought to have, the legislative powers in her own hands. England is, at this time, proudly coveting what would do her no good, were she to accomplish it; and the Continent hesitating on a matter, which will be her final ruin if neglected. It is the commerce and not the conquest of America, by which England is to be benefited, and that would in a great measure continue, were the countries as independant of each other as France and Spain; because in many articles, neither can go to a better market. But it is the independance of this country on Britain or any other, which is now the main and only object worthy of contention, and which, like all other truths discovered by necessity, will appear clearer and stronger every day.

First. Because it will come to that one time or other.

Secondly. Because, the longer it is delayed the harder it will be to accomplish.

I have frequently amused myself both in public and private companies, with silently remarking, the specious errors of those who speak without reflecting. And among the many which I have heard, the following seems most general, viz. that had this rupture happened forty or fifty years hence, instead of now, the Continent would have been more able to have shaken off the dependance. To which I reply, that our military ability at this time, arises from the experience gained in the last war, and which in forty or fifty years time, would have been totally extinct. The Continent, would not, by that time, have had a General, or even a military officer left; and we, or those who may succeed us, would have been as ignorant of martial matters as the ancient Indians: And this single position, closely attended to, will unanswerably prove, that the present time is preferable to all others. The argument turns thus— at the conclusion of the last war, we had experience, but wanted numbers; and forty or fifty years hence, we should have numbers, without experience; wherefore, the proper point of time, must be some particular point between the two extremes, in which a sufficiency of the former remains, and a proper increase of the latter is obtained: And that point of time is the present time.

The reader will pardon this digression, as it does not properly come under the head I first set out with, and to which I again return by the following position, viz.

Should affairs be patched up with Britain, and she to remain the governing and sovereign power of America, (which, as matters arenow circumstanced, is giving up the point entirely) we shall deprive ourselves of the very means of sinking the debt we have, or may contract. The value of the back lands which some of the provinces are clandestinely deprived of, by the unjust extension of the limits of Canada, valued only at five pounds sterling per hundred acres, amount to upwards of twenty – five millions, Pennsylvania currency; and the quit – rents at one penny sterling per acre, to two millions yearly.

It is by the sale of those lands that the debt may be sunk,

without burthen to any, and the quit – rent reserved thereon, will always lessen, and in time, will wholly support the yearly expence of government. It matters not how long the debt is in paying, so that the lands when sold be applied to the discharge of it, and for the execution of which, the Congress for the time being, will be the continental trustees.

I proceed now to the second head, viz. Which is the easiest and most practicable plan, RECONCILIATION or INDEPENDANCE; with some occasional remarks.

He who takes nature for his guide is not easily beaten out of his argument, and on that ground, I answer generally—That INDEPENDANCE being a SINGLE SIMPLE LINE, contained within ourselves; and reconciliation, a matter exceedingly perplexed and complicated, and in which, a treacherous capricious court is to interfere, gives the answer without a doubt.

The present state of America is truly alarming to every man who is capable of reflexion. Without law, without government, without any other mode of power than what is founded on, and granted by courtesy. Held together by an unexampled concurrence of sentiment, which, is nevertheless subject to change, and which, every secret enemy is endeavouring to dissolve. Our present condition, is, Legislation without law; wisdom without a plan; a constitution without a name; and, what is strangely astonishing, perfect Independance contending for dependance. The instance is without a precedent; the case never existed before; and who can tell what may be the event? The property of no man is secure in the present unbraced system of things. The mind of the multitude is left at random, and seeing no fixed object before them, they pursue such as fancy or opinion starts. Nothing is criminal; there is no such thing as treason; wherefore, every one thinks himself at liberty to act as he pleases. The Tories dared not have assembled offensively, had they known that their lives, by that act, were forfeited to the laws of the state. A line of distinction should be drawn, between, English soldiers taken in battle, and inhabitants of America taken in arms. The first are prisoners, but the latter traitors. The one forfeits his liberty, the other his head.

Notwithstanding our wisdom, there is a visible feebleness in some of our proceedings which gives encouragement to dissentions. The Continental Belt is too loosely buckled. And if something is not done in time, it will be too late to do any thing, and we shall fall into a state, in which, neither Reconciliation nor Independance will be practicable. The king and his worthless adherents are got at their old game of dividing the Continent, and there are not wanting among us, Printers, who will be busy spreading specious falsehoods. The artful and hypocritical letter which appeared a few months ago in two of the New – York papers, and likewise in two others, is an evidence that there are men who want either judgment or honesty.

It is easy getting into holes and corners and talking of reconciliation: But do such men seriously consider, how difficult the task is, and how dangerous it may prove, should the Continent divide thereon. Do they take within their view, all the various orders of men whose situation and circumstances, as well as their own, are to be considered therein. Do they put themselves in the place of the sufferer whose all is already gone, and of the soldier, who hath quitted all for the defence of his country. If their ill judged moderation be suited to their own private situations only, regardless of others, the event will convince them, that "they are reckoning without their Host. "

Put us, say some, on the footing we were on in sixty – three: To which I answer, the request is not now in the power of Britain to comply with, neither will she propose it; but if it were, and even should be granted, I ask, as a reasonable question, By what means is such a corrupt and faithless court to be kept to its engagements? Another parliament, nay, even the present, may hereafter repeal the obligation, on the pretence, of its being violently obtained, or unwisely granted; and in that case, Where is our redress? —No going to law with nations; cannon are the bar-

risters of Crowns; and the sword, not of justice, but of war, de-
cides the suit. To be on the footing of sixty – three, it is not sufficient, that the laws only be put on the same state, but, that our
circumstances, likewise, be put on the same state; Our burnt and
destroyed towns repaired or built up, our private losses made
good, our public debts (contracted for defence) discharged; otherwise, we shall be millions worse than we were at that enviable
period. Such a request, had it been complied with a year ago,
would have won the heart and soul of the Continent—but now it is
too late, "The Rubicon is passed. "

Besides, the taking up arms, merely to enforce the repeal of
a pecuniary law, seems as unwarrantable by the divine law, and
as repugnant to human feelings, as the taking up arms to enforce
obedience thereto. The object, on either side, doth not justify the
means; for the lives of men are too valuable to be cast away on
such trifles. It is the violence which is done and threatened to our
persons; the destruction of our property by an armed force; the
invasion of our country by fire and sword, which conscientiously
qualifies the use of arms: And the instant, in which such a mode
of defence became necessary, all subjection to Britain ought to
have ceased; and the independancy of America, should have
been considered, as dating its aera from, and published by, the
first musket that was fired against her. This line is a line of consis-

tency; neither drawn by caprice, nor extended by ambition; but produced by a chain of events, of which the colonies were not the authors.

I shall conclude these remarks, with the following timely and well intended hints. We ought to reflect, that there are three different ways, by which an independancy may hereafter be effected; and that one of those three, will one day or other, be the fate of America, viz. By the legal voice of the people in Congress; by a military power; or by a mob: It may not always happen that our soldiers are citizens, and the multitude a body of reasonable men; virtue, as I have already remarked, is not hereditary, neither is it perpetual. Should an independancy be brought about by the first of those means, we have every opportunity and every encouragement before us, to form the noblest purest constitution on the face of the earth. We have it in our power to begin the world over again. A situation, similar to the present, hath not happened since the days of Noah until now. The birthday of a new world is at hand, and a race of men, perhaps as numerous as all Europe contains, are to receive their portion of freedom from the event of a few months. The Reflexion is awful—and in this point of view, How trifling, how ridiculous, do the little, paltry cavellings, of a few weak or interested men appear, when weighed against the business of a world.

Should we neglect the present favorable and inviting period, and an Independance be hereafter effected by any other means, we must charge the consequence to ourselves, or to those rather, whose narrow and prejudiced souls, are habitually opposing the measure, without either inquiring or reflecting. There are reasons to be given in support of Independance, which men should rather privately think of, than be publicly told of. We ought not now to be debating whether we shall be independant or not, but, anxious to accomplish it on a firm, secure, and honorable basis, and uneasy rather that it is not yet began upon. Every day convinces us of its necessity. Even the Tories (if such beings yet remain among us) should, of all men, be the most solicitous to promote it; for, as the appointment of committees at first, protected them from popular rage, so, a wise and well established form of government, will be the only certain means of continuing it securely to them. Wherefore, if they have not virtue enough to be WHIGS, they ought to have prudence enough to wish for Independance.

In short, Independance is the only BOND that can tye and keep us together. We shall then see our object, and our ears will be legally shut against the schemes of an intriguing, as well, as a cruel enemy. We shall then too, be on a proper footing, to treat with Britain; for there is reason to conclude, that the pride of that court, will be less hurt by treating with the American states for terms of peace, than with those, whom she denominates, "rebel-lious subjects," for terms of accommodation. It is our delaying it that encourages her to hope for conquest, and our backwardness tends only to prolong the war. As we have, without any good effect therefrom, withheld our trade to obtain a redress of our griev-ances, let us now try the alternative, by independantly redressing them ourselves, and then offering to open the trade. The mercan-tile and reasonable part in England, will be still with us; be-cause, peace with trade, is preferable to war without it. And if this offer be not accepted, other courts may be applied to.

On these grounds I rest the matter. And as no offer hath yet been made to refute the doctrine contained in the former editions of this pamphlet, it is a negative proof, that either the doctrine cannot be refuted, or, that the party in favour of it are too numer-ous to be opposed. WHEREFORE, instead of gazing at each other with suspicious or doubtful curiosity, let each of us, hold out to his neighbour the hearty hand of friendship, and unite in drawing a line, which, like an act of oblivion, shall bury in forgetfulness every former dissention. Let the names of Whig and Tory be ex-tinct; and let none other be heard among us, than those of a good citizen, an open and resolute friend, and a virtuous supporter of the RIGHTS of MANKIND and of the FREE AND INDEPEN-DANT STATES OF AMERICA.

英国国王乔治三世对议会的演说

1775 年 10 月 27 日

　　当前美利坚的形势以及每于重要事项我皆希望征求诸位意见并获得诸位拥戴和支持的习惯使我决定今天很早就召见诸位，聚于一堂。

　　长期以来，有些人以严重误导之手段极力煽动我美利坚人民，向他们灌输其体制观念，严重破坏殖民地的政体及其与大不列颠的从属关系，现在这些人已经公开宣布反叛，进行敌对活动和造反。他们已经召集军队，组建海军力量，扣留公共税收，并试图构建立法、行政和司法机关。他们已经以最任意的司法方法处理他们同伴的人身和财产了。虽然许多不幸的人不赞成他们，保持对我忠诚并希望对他们加以抵制，但也可能受蒙蔽而不能看到此次反叛之致命后果，暴力之洪流已经如此强大并可能裹挟其他人屈从，直至有足够的力量出现支持拥戴我的这些臣民们。

制造和推动这种严重阴谋的人极大地利用了我们与他们意图不一致的因素。他们用似是而非的表述混淆视听，极力挑拨与母国之关系，严重诋毁人们对我本人的忠诚，同时在准备全面反叛。在我们这边，虽然你们在上次会议上已经宣布马萨诸塞海港地区存在反叛，即使对该地区，我们也只是希望重修旧好而不是加以制服。议会的决议体现了和解和宽容的精神，和解的建议应当结合有力措施加以实行，强制手段只适用于尚未武装反叛的臣民中的犯罪行为。我本着同样的态度，只要有可能，就急切防止我的臣民们流血，防止战争状态带来不可避免的灾难。我仍然希望我的美利坚子民们认清他们首领们的叛国念头，相信作为英国的臣民，在各个方面，都将是世界上有史以来最文明社会中最自由的成员。

他们挑起的反叛战争已经扩大化，并且公开宣称要继续下去，企图建立一个独立的国家。我无须详述此项图谋如果成功将带来的致命后果。鉴于兹事体大，鉴于英国的崇高精神，鉴于上帝赐予英国之丰富资源，我们不能放弃这些殖民地，英国花费了巨大精力开拓了殖民地工业，怀着极大的慈爱之情养育了殖民地，给予诸多商业优惠促进殖民地发展，并付出了巨大生命和财产的牺牲保护它们的安全。

现在以决断的方法迅捷结束动乱，才是智慧和宽容的表现（如果有效）。为此目的，我尽量以给我的王国最小负担的方式增加了我们的海军力量，扩大了我们的地面军力。

我欣慰地告知诸位，我已经收到外邦对我们提供支持的最友好提议。我如果就此签订条约，有关条约就能达成并送到你们面前。我发誓热爱我的人民，我对他们的利益感同身受，为了使本王国大部分的在编武装部队能够用于维持王国安全，以及国家军事力量能够平等地用于捍卫我的王室、保卫我的人民的权利和安全，我已经派出驻守直布罗陀和马洪港的卫戍部队，还可能采取进一步的军事行动。

如果不幸和受蒙骗的大众在大军抵达之时能够对他们的错误幡然悔悟，我将随时怀着温和慈爱的态度接受我的这些迷途的子民。为了避免因为他们所处位置遥远带来的不便，消除他们可能经受的苦难，我将授权指定之人到现场发布大赦或特赦。赦免方式和赦免对象皆得以他们认为最适宜的方式实施，并接受任何愿意重新归顺的地区和殖民地。我还可以授权这些人采取行动恢复这些地区或殖民的地秩序，使其回到过去的忠诚，进行自由贸易，并对迷途知返者给予同样的保护和安全，如同这些地区未曾反叛一样。

下议院的诸位先生们，

我已经下令对明年开支进行的适当评估并下发给你

们。我依靠你们对我的忠心，依靠你们维护这个国家的公平正义的决心，依靠你们提供支持以满足处理当前形势所需。在这次反叛带来的众多难以避免的后果中，最使我痛心的是不得不增加我忠实的臣民们的额外负担。

我的勋爵们和先生们，

我对你们完全坦陈我的想法和意图。我长期所思所想和最迫切的愿望就是衷心希望我的所有臣民都平安幸福，我治下的地区恢复秩序和安宁，大家紧密团结、互相依靠。你们已经知悉现在动乱的趋势，我也告知你们，我为了制止动乱而采取的措施。为了达到此项目的，请诸位考虑还有哪些事情需要进行。我依赖你们的智慧。另外，我高兴补充，从我收到的保证和出于欧洲事务的总体考虑方面看，我认为你们采取的措施不会引起任何外国政府的干涉。

King George Ⅲ's Speech to Parliament
October 27, 1775

THE present situation of America, and my constant desire to have your advice, concurrence and assistance, on every important occasion, have determined me to call you thus early together.

Those who have long too successfully laboured to inflame

my people in America by gross misrepresentations, and to infuse into their minds a system of opinions, repugnant to the true constitution of the colonies, and to their subordinate relation to Great – Britain, now openly avow their revolt, hostility and rebellion. They have raised troops, and are collecting a naval force; they have seized the public revenue, and assumed to themselves legislative, executive and judicial powers, which they already exercise in the most arbitrary manner, over the persons and property of their fellow – subjects: And altho's many of these unhappy people may still retain their loyalty, and may be too wise not to see the fatal consequence of this usurpation, and wish to resist it, yet the torrent of violence has been strong e-nough to compel their acquiescence, till a sufficient force shall appear to support them.

The authors and promoters of this desperate conspiracy have, in the conduct of it, derived great advantage from the difference of our intentions and theirs. They meant only to amuse by vague expressions of attachment to the Parent State, and the strongest protestations of loyalty to me, whilst they were preparing for a general revolt. On our part, though it was declared in your last session that a rebellion existed within the province of the Massachusetts Bay, yet even that province we wished rather to reclaim than to subdue.

The resolutions of Parliament breathed a spirit of moderation and forbearance; conciliatory propositions accompanied the
measures taken to enforce authority; and the coercive acts were
adapted to cases of criminal combinations amongst subjects not
then in arms. I have acted with the same temper; anxious to prevent, if it had been possible, the effusion of the blood of my
subjects; and the calamities which are inseparable from a state
of war; still hoping that my people in America would have dis-
cerned the traitorous views of their leaders, and have been convinced, that to be a subject of Great Britain, with all its consequences, is to be the freest member of any civil society in the
known world.

The rebellious war now levied is become more general, and
is manifestly carried on for the purpose of establishing an independent empire. I need not dwell upon the fatal effects of the
success of such a plan. The object is too important, the spirit of
the British nation too high, the resources with which God hath
blessed her too numerous, to give up so many colonies which
she has planted with great industry, nursed with great tenderness, encouraged with many commercial advantages, and protected and defended at much expence of blood and treasure.

It is now become the part of wisdom, and (in its effects)
of clemency, to put a speedy end to these disorders by the most

decisive exertions. For this purpose, I have increased my naval establishment, and greatly augmented my land forces; but in such a manner as may be the least burthensome to my kingdoms.

I have also the satisfaction to inform you, that I have received the most friendly offers of foreign assistance; and if I shall make any treaties in consequence thereof, they shall be laid before you. And I have, in testimony of my affection for my people, who can have no cause in which I am not equally interested, sent to the garrisons of Gibraltar and Port – Mahon a part of my electoral troops, in order that a larger number of the established forces of this kingdom may be applied to the maintenance of its authority; and the national militia, planned and regulated with equal regard to the rights, safety and protection of my crown and people, may give a farther extent and activity to our military operations.

When the unhappy and deluded multitude, against whom this force will be directed, shall become sensible of their error, I shall be ready to receive the misled with tenderness and mercy, and in order to prevent the inconveniencies which may arise from the great distance of their situation, and to remove as soon as possible the calamities which they suffer, I shall give authority to certain persons upon the spot to grant general or particular pardons and indemnities, in such manner, and to such persons as they shall think fit; and to receive the submission of any Province or Colony which shall be disposed to return to its allegiance. It may be also proper to authorise the persons so commissioned to restore such Province or Colony, so returning to its allegiance, to the free exercise of its trade and commerce, and to the same protection and security as if such Province or Colony had never revolted.

Gentlemen of the House of Commons,

I have ordered the proper estimates for the ensuing year to be laid before you; and I rely on your affection to me, and your resolution to maintain the just rights of this country, for such supplies as the present circumstances of our affairs require. Among the many unavoidable ill consequences of this rebellion, none affects me more sensibly than the extraordinary burthen which it must create to my faithful subjects.

My Lords, and Gentlemen,

I have fully opened to you my views and intentions. The constant employment of my thoughts, and the most earnest wishes of my heart, tend wholly to the safety and happiness of all my people, and to the reestablishment of order and tranquility through the several parts of my dominions, in a close connection and constitutional dependance. You see the tendency of the present disorders, and I have stated to you the measures which I mean to pursue for suppressing them. Whatever remains to be done, that may farther contribute to this end, I commit to your wisdom. And I am happy to add, that, as well from the assurances I have received, as from the general appearances of affairs in Europe, I see no probability that the measures which you may adopt will be interrupted by disputes with any foreign power.

美国独立宣言[120]

(1776 年 7 月 4 日在费城召开的第二届大陆会议上通过)

作者：杰斐逊[121] 等

在人类事业之中，当一部分人有必要与束缚他们的另一群体解除政治联系，并按照自然法则和上帝授予他们的权利，获得以独立平等的身份立于世界列国之林时，出于

---

[120] 全名为《美利坚十三邦一致同意之宣言》（THE UNANIMOUS DE-CLARATION OF THE THIRTEEN UNITED STATES OF AMERAICA）。北美十三邦（美国建国之后，中文翻译时通常将"邦（State）"译为"州"。它们指英国于1607 年（弗吉尼亚）至 1733 年（佐治亚）在北美洲大西洋沿岸建立的一系列殖民地。这些殖民地最终成为美利坚合众国独立时的组成部分。这些殖民地分别是特拉华、宾夕法尼亚、新泽西、佐治亚、康涅狄格、马萨诸塞、马里兰、南卡罗来纳、新罕布什尔、弗吉尼亚、纽约、北卡罗来纳和罗德岛，每个殖民地都建立并发展了自治体制，居民大多数是拥有自己土地的独立农民。

[121] 托马斯·杰斐逊（1743～1826），生于弗吉尼亚的一个富裕家庭。曾就读于威廉-玛丽学院。1767 年成为律师，1769 年当选为弗吉尼亚下院议员。他积极投身于独立运动之中，并代表弗吉尼亚出席大陆会议。他曾两次当选弗吉尼亚州长。1800 年当选美国总统。杰斐逊起草了《独立宣言》的第一稿，富兰克林等人又进行了润色。大陆会议对此稿又进行了长时间的、激烈的辩论，最终作出了重大的修改。特别是在佐治亚和卡罗来纳代表们的坚持下，删去了杰斐逊对英王乔治三世允许殖民地保持奴隶制和奴隶买卖的有力谴责。这一部分的原文是这样的："他的人性本身发动了残酷的战争，侵犯了一个从未冒犯过他的远方民族的最神圣的生存权和自由权；他诱骗他们，并把他们运往另一半球充当奴隶，或使他们惨死在运送途中。"

对人类见解之尊重，他们应当宣布促使他们分立之原因。

我们认为这些真理是不言而喻的：人人生而平等，造物主赋予他们若干不可剥夺之权利，其中包括生命、自由和追求幸福之权。为了保障这些权利，人们才在他们中间建立政府，而政府的正当权力来自于被管理者们的同意。当任何形式的政府成为对这些目标的破坏时，人民便有权予以更换或废除，并建立一个新的政府。新政府遵循的原则和其权力配置的模式，应当使人民认为唯有这样才最有可能使他们获得安全和幸福。诚然，兹事体大，出于慎重，成立多年的政府不应当因为一些轻微的和暂时的原因而予以更换。鉴于此种考虑，一切经验表明：人类情愿忍受苦难，只要恶行尚能忍受，而不太愿意诉诸他们的权利废除他们已经习惯的政府。然而，当一个政府一贯滥用职权、强取豪夺、坚持其一贯目标，显然欲置人民于长期专制暴政之下，人民就有权利，也有责任推翻这种政府，并为他们的未来安全设立新的保障。这就是这些殖民地人民长期以来忍受的苦难，也是他们现在不得不改变旧政权制度的原因。当今大不列颠国王的历史，就是屡屡伤害和掠夺这些殖民地的历史，其直接目标就是要建立独裁暴政凌驾于我等各邦。为了证明以上陈述，兹向世界上的正义诸君提交下列事实：

他拒绝批准对公众利益最有益和最必需的法律。

他禁止他的殖民地总督批准刻不容缓、极端重要的法律，除非这些法律延缓执行，直至得到他的同意，然而这些法律延缓以后，他又完全置之不理。

他拒绝批准广大地区人民安置相关的其他法律，除非这些地区的人民情愿放弃在立法机构中的代表权；而代表权对人民是无比珍贵的，只有暴君才有所畏惧。

他总是将立法委员召集到异乎寻常、极不舒适而又远离他们的公共记录存放之地去开会，唯一的目的仅是使他们疲惫不堪而被迫同意他的措施。

他一再解散众议院，皆因代表们坚决反对他侵犯人民之权利。

他在解散众议院之后，又长期拒绝另选他人，以致此项不可或缺之立法权不能正常行使，从而已经重回大众之手各行其是，此等状况延续日久致使各邦处于外敌入侵和内部骚乱种种危险境地。

他努力阻止各邦增加人口，为此目的，他设置障碍阻止制定外国人归化法，拒绝通过其他法律鼓励移民，并提高分配新土地的条件。

他拒绝同意确立司法权力的法律，阻挠司法之执行。

他迫使法官们为了保住任期、薪金的数额和领取而只服从于他个人意志。

他滥设众多机构，委派成群的官员到此骚扰我们的人民，吞噬人民之财物。

他在和平时期，未经我们立法机构同意，就在我们中间维持其常备军队。

他施加影响，使军队不受民政之节制，并凌驾于民政权力之上。

他同别人勾结，置我等于不符合我们法制亦未经我们法律承认的司法管辖之下，并对伪立法机构之各种法案予以批准，从而达到以下目的：

在我们中间驻扎大批武装部队；

为保护他们，不论这些人对我各邦居民犯下何等严重的谋杀罪，皆得以徒有形式之审理逃脱惩处；

切断我们同世界各地的贸易；

未经我们同意便向我们征税；

在许多案件中剥夺我们享有陪审团审理的权利；

以莫须有的罪名把我们押送海外受审；

在一个邻近地区废除了英国法律中的自由制度，在那里建立专制政府，扩大其疆域，使其立即成为一个样板和合适的工具，以便向这里各殖民地推行同样的专制统治；

取消我们的宪章，废除我们最珍贵的法律并从根本上改变我们各邦政府的形式；

中止我们立法机构行使权力，宣称他们被授予在任何情况下为我们制定法律的权力。

他否定我们政府之地位，宣称我们已不属他保护之列，并向我们发动战争。

他在我们的海域里大肆掠夺，蹂躏我们的沿海地区，烧毁我们的城镇，残害我们人民的生命。

他此时正在运送大批外国雇佣兵至此，以完成其未竟之制造死亡、荒凉和暴政的勾当。此种种恶行已由他而始，其残忍卑劣之程度即使于最野蛮的时代亦罕有其配，他已完全不配当一个文明国家的元首。

他强迫在公海上被他们俘虏的我们的同胞拿起武器反对自己的国家，使他们成为残杀自己亲友的刽子手，或使他们死于自己亲友的手下。

他在我们中间煽动内乱，将我边疆居民带入残酷无情的印第安蛮族屠杀之险境，而已知印第安人作战的规则是不分男女老幼、是非曲直，格杀勿论。

在遭受这些压迫的每一阶段，我们都曾以最谦卑的言辞请愿补救。而我们屡次请愿，皆被报以伤害。如此君主，其所作所为皆显示其为暴君，实不堪为我自由人民之统治者。

长期以来，我等对英国同胞关注有加。我们一直在警示他们，其立法机关企图将无根据之管辖权扩展到我们这里，我们时常提醒他们此间我们移民定居情况。我们也曾诉诸他们天性中之正义感和高尚情怀，恳求他们念在同种同宗的份上，弃绝这些掠夺行为，因为这些掠夺行为必致使我们之间的关系和来往中断。可他们对同胞们的正当呼声也充耳不闻。因此，我们不得不确认有必要与他们分离，以对待世界上其他民族的态度对待他们：于交战时为敌人，于和平时为朋友。

我等美利坚合众国的代表们聚集于大陆会议，诉诸世界最高裁判以判明我等意图正义，谨以各殖民地善良人民的名义，并经其授权，庄严宣告：这些联合起来的殖民地从此是，而且有权应该是，自由独立之国家；它们解除与英国王室一切附属关系，解除所有与大不列颠王国之间的一切政治联系，它们有全权享有宣战、缔结和平盟约、建立商务关系，以及采取独立国家有权采取的一切行为。我们坚定地信赖神明保佑，以生命、财产和神圣的名誉彼此宣誓保证拥护此项宣言。

（各州代表签名从略）

The Declaration of Independence
IN CONGRESS, JULY 4, 1776

When in the course of human events, it becomes necessary for one people to dissolve the political bands which have connected them with another, and to assume among the powers of the earth, the separate and equal station to which the laws Nature and Nature's God entitle them, a decent respect to the opinions of mankind requires that they should declare the causes which impel them to the separation.

We hold these truths to be self – evident, that all men are created equal, that they are endowed by their Creator with certain unalienable rights, that they are among these are life, liberty and the pursuit of happiness. That to secure these rights, governments are instituted among them, deriving their just power from the consent of the governed. That whenever any form of government becomes destructive of these ends, it is the right of the people to alter or to abolish it, and to institute new government, laying its foundation on such principles and organizing its powers in such form, as to them shall seem most likely to effect their safety and happiness. Prudence, indeed, will dictate that governments long established should not be changed for light and transient causes; and accordingly all experience hath shown that mankind are more disposed to suffer, while evils are sufferable, than to right themselves by abolishing the forms to which they are accustomed. But when a long train of abuses and usurpations, pursuing invariably the same object, evinces a design to reduce them under absolute despotism, it is their right, it is their duty, to throw off such government, and to provide new guards for their future security. Such has been the patient sufferance of these Colonies; and such is now the necessity, which constrains them to alter their former systems of government. The history of the present King of Great Britain is usurpations, all having in direct object tyranny over these States. To prove this, let facts be submitted to a candid world.

He has refused his assent to laws, the most wholesome and necessary for the public good.

He has forbidden his Governors to pass laws of immediate and pressing importance, unless suspended in their operation till his assent should be obtained; and when so suspended, he has utterly neglected to attend them.

He has refused to pass other laws for the accommodation of large districts of people, unless those people would relinquish the right of representation in the Legislature, a right inestimable to them and formidable to tyrants only.

He has called together legislative bodies at places unusual, uncomfortable, and distant from the depository of their public records, for the sole purpose of fatiguing them into compliance with his measures.

He has dissolved representative houses repeatedly, for opposing with manly firmness his invasion on the rights of the people.

He has refused for a long time, after such dissolution, to cause others to be elected ; whereby the legislative powers, incapable of annihilation, have returned to the people at large for their exercise; the State remaining in the meantime exposed to all the dangers of invasion from without and convulsion within.

He has endeavored to prevent the population of these states; for that purpose obstructing the laws of naturalizing of foreigners; refusing to pass others to encourage their migration hither, and raising the condition of new appropriations of lands.

He has obstructed the administration of justice, by refusing his assent of laws for establishing judiciary powers.

He has made judges dependent on his will alone, for the tenure of their office, and the amount and payment of their salary.

He has erected a multitude of new officers, and sent hither swarms of officers to harass our people, and eat out our substances.

He has kept among us, in times of peace, standing armies without the consent of our legislatures.

He has affected to render the military independent of and superior to the civil power.

He has combined with others to subject us to a jurisdiction foreign to our constitution, and unacknowledged by our laws; giving his assent to their acts of pretended legislation.

For quartering large bodies of armed troops among us;

For protecting them, by a mock trial, from punishment for any murder which they should commit on the inhabitants of these States.

For cutting off our trade with all parts of the world;

For imposing taxes on us without our consent;

For depriving us in many cases, of the benefits of trial by jury;

For transporting us beyond seas to be tried for pretended offenses;

For abolishing the free systems of English laws in a neighboring Province, establishing therein an arbitrary government, and enlarging its boundaries so as to render it at once an example and fit instrument for introducing the same absolute rule these Colonies;

For taking away our Charters, abolishing our most valuable laws, and altering fundamentally the forms of our governments;

For suspending our own Legislatures, and declaring themselves invested with power to legislate for us in all cases whatsoever.

He has abdicated government here, by declaring us out of his protection and waging war against us.

He has plundered our seas, ravaged our coasts, burnt our towns, and destroyed the lives of our people.

He is at this time transporting large armies of foreign mercenaries to complete the works of death, desolation and tyranny, already begun with circumstances of cruelty and perfidy scarcely parallel in the most barbarous ages, and totally unworthy the head of a civilized nation.

He has constrained our fellow citizens taken captive on the high seas to bear arms against their country, to become the executioners of their friends and brethren, or to fall themselves by their hands.

He has excited domestic insurrection amongst us, and has endeavored to bring on the inhabitants of our frontiers, the merciless Indian savages, whose known rule of warfare, is an undistinguished destruction of all ages, sexes, and conditions.

In every stage of these oppressions we have petitioned for redress in the most humble terms: our repeated petition have been answered only by repeated injury. A prince whose character is thus marked by every act which may define a tyrant is unfit to be the ruler of a free people.

Nor have we been wanting in attention to our British brethren. We have warned them from time to time of attempts by their legislature to extend an unwarrantable jurisdiction over us. We have reminded them of the circumstances of our emigration and settlement here. We have appealed to their native justice and magnanimity, and we have conjured them by the ties of our common kindred to disavow these usurpation, which would inevitably interrupt our connections and correspondence. They too have been deaf to the voice of justice and of consanguinity. We must, therefore, acquiesce in the necessity, which denounces our separation, and hold them, as we hold the rest of mankind, enemies in war, in peace friends.

We, therefore, the Representatives of the United States of America, in General Congress assembled, appealing to the supreme Judge of the world for the rectitude of our intentions, do, in the name, and by authority of the good people of these Colonies, solemnly publish and declare, that these United States Colonies are, and of right to be, free and Independent States; that they are absolved by from all allegiance to the British Crown, and that all political connection between them and the State, they have full power to levy war, conclude peace, contract alliances, establish commerce, and to do all other acts and things which Independent States may of right do. And for the support of this declaration, with a firm reliance on the protection of Divine Providence, we mutually pledge to each other our lives, our fortunes, and our sacred honor.